SHARIA & POLITICS

WRITTEN BY **QAZI FAZL ULLAH**

EDITED BY **EVELYN THOMPSON**

HUND INTERNATIONAL PUBLISHING

LOS ANGELES, CALIFORNIA

2022

COPYRIGHT © 2022 BY QAZI FAZL ULLAH

All rights reserved. This book or any portion thereof may not be reproduced or used in any manner whatsoever without the express written permission of the publisher except for the use of brief quotations in a book review or scholarly journal.

FIRST PRINTING: 2022

ISBN: 978-1-970049-23-7

HUND INTERNATIONAL PUBLISHING

LOS ANGELES, CALIFORNIA

PRINTED IN THE UNITED STATES OF AMERICA

"BEHOLD! HIS (ALLAH) IS THE CREATION AND HIS IS THE RULE." (7:54)

Also by Qazi Fazl Ullah

Sharia & Politics

Science of Hadith

Jesus in the Quran

Jihad: Why, How, & When

Sayyidah Aaisha: Age & Marriage

Ramadan: Components of the Holy Month

Table of Contents

PREFACE	13
ALLAH THE CREATOR AND HIS CREATURE	18
ISLAM IS DEEN	23
ALLAH IS THE LAWGIVER	28
DEEN, SHARIA, AND FIQH	31
NECESSITY IS AUTHORITY	32
1. AUTHORITY IS PERMISSIBLE BUT NOT A MUST	33
2. THE SECOND OPINION IS THAT AUTHORITY AND LEADERSHIP IS ARE MUST AND THEREFORE MANDATORY.	33
KHALAFAH	41
TYPES OF GOVERNMENTS	48
SECULARISM	50
HOW AND WHY WAS SECULARISM INTRODUCED AND ADOPTED?	55
ISLAMIC SYSTEM OF GOVERNMENT	58
THE SOURCES OF ISLAMIC LAW	60
(I) FUNDAMENTAL SOURCES	60
(II) SECONDARY SOURCES	61
THE SOURCE OF KHILAFAH	63
HOW TO APPOINT AND DETERMINE SOMEONE FOR KHALAFAH?	66
AHLUL HALLI WAL AQD	79
REQUIRED QUALITIES OF A KHALIFA	81
1. MUST BE A MUSLIM	81
2. MUST BE ADL	82

(III)	TO BE A JURIST	83
(IV)	TO HAVE STRONG WILLPOWER	84
(V)	SKILLED IN MILITARY STRATEGY AND TACTICS	84
(VI)	BE A GOOD POLITICAL PLANNER	84
(VII)	HE MUST BE MALE	84
(VIII)	HE MUST BE SOUND IN MIND AND BODY	87
(IX)	LINEAGE	90

AHLUSH SHURA — 92

IS THE SHURA'S ADVICE ON THE KHALIFA BINDING? — 97

AHLUL IJTIHAD — 102

RIGHTS AND DUTIES OF THE KHALIFA — 104

DUTIES OF KHALIFA — 105

A.	PROTECTION OF DEEN	105
B.	TO ESTABLISH A JUSTICE SYSTEM	105
C.	TO PROTECT THE STATE AND TO PROVIDE AND ESTABLISH PEACE	106
D.	TO CARRY OUT PUNISHMENT ON CRIMINALS	107
E.	TO PROTECT THE BOUNDARIES OF THE STATE	108
F.	STRIVING HARD AGAINST THOSE WHO CONSPIRE AGAINST ISLAM	109
G.	TO ESTABLISH EXCHEQUER (BAITUL MAL)	109
I.	HE MAY LISTEN TO SINCERE ADVICE FIRST	115
1.	FOOD, CLOTHING, AND SHELTER	117
2.	TO PROVIDE MEDICAL TREATMENT	117
3.	EDUCATION	118
4.	EMPLOYMENT AND JOBS	121
5.	ESTABLISH TRANSPORTATION INFRASTRUCTURE	123

6.	TO MAKE MARRIAGE EASIER	124

RIGHTS OF THE KHALIFA — 126

DUTIES AND RESPONSIBILITIES OF THE CITIZEN — 131

- A. TO ESTABLISH KHALAFAH — 131
- B. TO OBEY THE RULES AND LAWS — 132

RIGHTS OF THE CITIZENS — 149

- A. IN ISLAM, FIVE THINGS ARE VERY VALUABLE AND PRECIOUS, AND THESE ARE — 151
  - (I) LIFE — 151
  - (II) PROPERTY — 151
  - (III) FAITH AND RELIGION — 151
  - (IV) HONOR — 151
  - (V) KNOWLEDGE AND INTELLECT — 152
- B. RIGHT OF FREEDOM — 152
- C. THE RIGHT TO ACQUIRE BASIC NEEDS — 152
- D. THE RIGHT OF OWNERSHIP AND POSSESSION — 152
- E. THE RIGHT TO EDUCATION — 153
- F. THE RIGHT OF EXPRESSION/FREEDOM OF THOUGHT AND FREEDOM OF SPEECH — 154
- G. THE RIGHT OF CONSCIOUSNESS / RIGHT OF RELIGIOUS CONVICTION — 155
- H. THE RIGHT OF FREE MOVEMENTS AND MIGRATION — 156
- I. THE RIGHTS OF ASSOCIATION — 157
- J. THE RIGHT OF JUSTICE — 158
- K. THE RIGHT OF PROTEST — 158

MORE THAN ONE KHALIFA — 160

THE CHARACTERISTICS OF THE ISLAMIC SYSTEM — 163

1. ALLAH IS THE RULER AND QURAN AND SUNNAH ARE THE SUPREME LAW — 163

2.	THE RELATION OF INDIVIDUALS AMONGST THEM AND WITH THE STATE AND SOCIETY	164
3.	THE RULERS ARE FROM THE UMMAH	165
4.	ETHICAL AND MORAL EDUCATION OF THE NATION	166
5.	GOVERNMENT BY THE WILL OF PEOPLE BUT WITH CONDITIONS	166

THE CHARACTERISTICS OF THE ISLAMIC STATE — 168

ADMINISTRATION — 173

RESPONSIBILITIES OF THE PEOPLE APPOINTED BY THE KHALIFA — 175

JUDICIARY — 184

THE QUALITIES OF THE JUDGES — 187

- (I) TO BE ADL AND JUST — 188
- (II) THE JUDGE HAS TO BE A MAN — 188
- (III) THE TALENT AND CAPABILITY OF IJTIHAD ARE OTHER REQUIREMENTS OF A QADI ACCORDING TO THREE SCHOOLS OF JURISPRUDENCE AND SOME HANAFIS ALSO — 189

THE TYPES OF JUDGES — 192

THE APPOINTMENT OF JUDGES — 195

TAHKEEM (ARBITRATION) — 199

WILAYATUL MAZALIM — 201

AL HISBAH (OMBUDSMAN) — 205

THE COMPARISON BETWEEN JUDICIARY, WILAYTUL MAZALIM AND HISBAH — 211

THE RESEMBLANCE BETWEEN JUDICIARY AND HISBAH — 212

THE COMPARISON BETWEEN HISBAH AND WILAYATUL MAZALIM — 214

INTERNATIONAL RELATIONS	*216*
REMOVAL OF KHALIFA	*226*
WITH HIS DEATH	226
WITH HIS RESIGNATION	226
WITH REMOVAL	226
DEFECT IN BODY	227
BOOKS BY QAZI FAZL ULLAH	*233*
ABOUT THE AUTHOR	*246*

PREFACE

Human by nature is animalistic and social as well. As animals have desires, so do humans, and humans are social animals. Humans should not be forced to compromise on either desire or on sociology. Human sociology is based on intellect, but it is greatly influenced by living in a world of desires. So, most of the time, people use intellect and reason to fulfill these desires. Animals also have desires, and to fulfill them, an animal struggles, and may even attack other animals as well. It may also attack when defending itself or its desires. So having desires and defense are both part of its nature. Human beings do the same and use his intellect for desires and defense. Unfortunately, people often use power excessively and if an authority cannot control them, this excessive use brings disaster and turmoil. Allah said:

> *"Fasad [mischief/disorder/corruption] has appeared [or has overtaken] on land and sea because of what the hands of people have done, in order to cause to taste some of what they have done so they may make a U-turn." - (30:41)*

As we know, Allah has appointed humanity as His agent on earth. So, on one hand, people can utilize this world and exploit it. On the other, however, they are bound to obey Allah's commandments and to act accordingly. For this purpose, Allah sent prophets and messengers and gave them books and scriptures and inspired them with his rules and laws. Allah said:

> *"We have enjoined for you people the Deen which He (Allah) had enjoined to Noah and that one which we have inspired to you and that one which we had enjoined to Abraham, Moses, and Jesus to establish/keep straight and do not make Tafarruq [sects] pick and choose therein." - (42:13)*

So, Allah ordered its implementation. Also, Allah said:

> *"Indeed we had sent our messengers with clear proof (rules and laws), and we had sent down with them the scripture and the balance so humans may keep up justice." - (57:25)*

Allah continued:

> *"Verily we did send down the Torah in which there was guidance and light, by which the prophets who submitted themselves [to it] used to judge the Jews and their rabbis and the priests [also used it to pass judgement] as the book of Allah was entrusted to them and they were witnesses to that" - (5:44)*

Then Allah said:

> *"And we have sent down to you (O' Muhammad!) the book [Quran] in truth confirming the scriptures that came before it. So judge between them what Allah has revealed and follow not their vain desires, diverging away from the truth that has come to you. For each*

among you, we have prescribed a law and a clear way." - (5:48)

Allah said:

"Then we have put you (O' Muhammad) on a plain way (clear system and law) of Amr (Deen) so follow this and do not follow the vein desires of those who do not understand." - (45:18)

Also, Allah said:

"And whosoever did not judge on (the basis of) what Allah has sent down they disbelievers." – (5:44)

"they are wrongdoers." – (5:45)

"...they are rebellious." - (5:47)

It is logical that any machine or product will operate properly when the manufacturer's instructions are followed. Allah is not only the manufacturer or the inventor but also the Creator of the whole world, and He is the Lord of it as well. He has subjugated the world to humans and given them honor. Allah said:

"And indeed we have honored the children of Adam, and we have put them (as authority) in the land and sea." - (17:70)

Moreover, they are bound to obey and follow His commandments and to implement His laws and rules, and that is the proper operation of this world and worldly system.

When a machine is expensive and complicated, the manufacturing company does not simply send a manual with it. They send a representative to install it, to operate it, and to train and teach others to operate it. Similarly, Allah sent the Messengers and the scripture to make human life fruitful and useful now and in the hereafter.

This means that Islam, the *Deen* of Allah, is a system and code of life. Allah has sent to be implemented as the law of the land; in other words, we say that Islam is a complete and perfect political system. There is no other *Deen* in the world known for its political system; the rest of the world's governments are secular system. Moreover, if a government were to attempt to declare itself religious, then would be labeled as fundamentalism and be roundly condemned and opposed.

Both Muslims and non-Muslims pray and fast. However, Muslims claim to be liberal, moderate, people of the modern world, educated and learned as well. Why? Because they do not have knowledge or they might have only a little knowledge, but they are impressed by the scientific advancement of the secular world, and they are scared of expressing their view. Yes, not to express is one thing but if they do not believe that Islam is a system or express another way around then, they should think of their Iman whether it remains intact.

Sometimes some people are misguided due to certain circumstances. Otherwise, they are good Muslims if they will understand the issue. These are educated people and English, the most popular language of the developed world, impresses them. So as a *naseehah* (thinking, intending, looking for the best for them) we thought that we should write a book in English.

The Prophet of Allah said,

> *"Mankind is a mine, like the mines of gold and silver, the best one in [the time of] ignorance is the one in [the time of] Islam when they understood."* (Muslim)

Some 25 years ago we wrote a book in Urdu on the Islamic political system, so now we intend to write it in English, but with further details. May Allah (SWT) make it a genuine effort and a benefit for humans in general and for these Muslims mentioned above specifically, as they deserve this because they are good people (*Ameen*).

ALLAH THE CREATOR AND HIS CREATURE

Allah (Subhanahu Wa Ta'ala) is the sole creator of the world; those who did not believe in his oneness and Lordship when Allah said knew it:

> *"And if you (O' Muhammad) would have asked them (the disbelievers) who has created the heavens and the earth and subjected the sun and the moon? They would have surely said, Allah."* - (29:61)

Even the atheist cannot attribute this creation to any other creature. They will either say that it came into existence automatically, which does not make any sense, or they will say some unknown power has created it. However, they do not believe that that power is Allah, and neither do we, but for different reasons. Since Allah created this world, he is behind the smooth running of it as well. It does not make sense that he created it and it is automatically running by itself.

In the world of technology, there are one must look at the websites, computer systems that support them, the satellite systems that support the computers, and so on. Moreover, within a computer there is a control command, operation system, etc., which the computer scientists are looking after every minute. Through that, they look after every connection connected to the control system. This is only an example to understand that Allah is Allah. He is looking after His creatures every single minute and second. Allah said:

> "And with Him [Allah] are the keys of Ghaib [everything that is unknown to humans] no one knows them but He alone and He knows whatever is there on the earth and in the sea and not even a leaf falls, but He knows it and not even a [small] grain in the darkness of the earth nor wet [fresh] or dry [old] that is in a clear record (in his knowledge)." - (6:59)

Allah said:

> "And nothing is hidden from your Lord even the weight [or volume] of an atom on the earth or in the heaven. Nor what is less [smaller] than that or bigger but that is in the clear record." - (10:61)

Allah said:

> "Not even a small atom can hide from Him [Allah] in the heaven or the earth, and not less than that is bigger but that is in the clear record." - (34:3)

> "And indeed We have created above you seven heavens, and we are not unaware of our creature (even for a second but We watch it)." - (23:17)

However, a king has workers working for him in his name and he needs them, for he cannot take care of everything himself. Allah does not need anyone but still as a Lord and King, He has the appointed the angels for certain duties and they have their networks or spheres of influence, which Muslims visualize as webs. Allah said:

> *"They [the angels] do not disobey whatever Allah has commanded them, but they do whatever they have been ordered." - (66:6)*

Regarding this web Allah said,

> *"And by the heavens full of paths [webs]." - (51:7)*

Allah has two types of laws:

Takweeni or natural laws: all creation is subject to these rules and laws in such a way that they cannot be averted it or avoided.

Allah said:

> *"And you can never find any aversion for the* Sunnah *[natural law] of Allah." - (35:43)*

> *"And you cannot find any change for the* Sunnah *of Allah" (33:62).*

In English, we say, "Let nature take its course." So, day and night come in alternation; the sun and the moon float in their orbits. Allah said:

> *"And a sign for them is the night, we withdrew there from the day and behold then they are in darkness, and the Sun runs on its fixed course for [an appointed] term. That is the decree [or controlling authority] of the Almighty, the all knower. And the moon we have measured for its mansion till it returns like the old dried curved date stalk. It is not for the sun to overtake the moon, nor does the night outstep the day; they all flow in an orbit. - (36:37-40)*

Human beings, like all other creatures, are also subject to the same law without having any free will in this regard. So, they become hungry and thirsty; they must relieve themselves; they fall asleep; they become sick. Allah said:

> "And among his signs is the creation of the heavens and the earth and the difference of your languages and colors, indeed in that there are signs for people. And among his signs is your sleep at night and day and your seeking of his bounty [as you feel hungry and thirsty, and you look for food and water)) indeed in that there are signs for people who listen." - (30:22-23)

Tashree'i laws: As Allah subjugated the whole world to humans, and they exploit it for their good and benefit, so He subjected them to his laws and rule and gave them free will as a test. If they pass the test, they are the successful people; if not, they are the losers.

Allah said:

> "And by the Asr *(time)* indeed human beings suffered great loss except those who believed and practiced righteous good deeds and enjoined one another with truth and enjoined one another with patience [stability and steadfastness]." (103:1-3)

Allah has given humans the ability to do right or wrong.

Allah said:

> "And by the nature and its perfect proportion. So he inspired it with its evils and piety." (91:7-8)

He showed them the path naturally and through a message. Allah said:

> "Indeed we showed him the path whether to be grateful or ungrateful." - (63:3)

Allah said:

> "[We sent] Messengers as givers of glad tidings and as to warn people, so Mankind may not have any plea against Allah after these Messengers. And Allah is almighty and all-wise." - (4:165)

Now Allah has the perfect plea. Allah said:

> "Say [O' Muhammad] then only for Allah is the perfect plea and if he would have willed [as a Takween], he would have guided you all [forcefully by Takween]." - (6:149)

Now that is for people to believe or to disbelieve. Allah said:

> "And say [O' Muhammad] [this is] the truth from your Lord, and then whoever wills let him believe and whoever wills let him disbelieve." - (18:29)

Allah said:

> "If you disbelieve then verily Allah is not in your need. He likes not disbelief for his slaves. And if you are grateful He pleases that for you." - (39:7)

So, Allah has made the Whole world subject to humans, and He has made them subject to his laws and system to believe in, to follow it, and to implement it as well. That is the true meaning of "Rabb" and "Abd" which means Lord and slave.

ISLAM IS DEEN

(I) "ISLAM" IS THE *DEEN* OF ALLAH

Allah said:

> "*Surely to Allah belongs the pure* Deen.*"* - *(39:3)*

(II) THE DEEN OF ALL THE MESSENGERS

Allah said:

> "*He [Allah] has ordained for you the same* Deen *[Islam] which he ordained for Noah, and that one which we have inspired to you [O Muhammad] and that one which we ordained for Abraham, Moses, and Jesus, that implement this* Deen *and do not make sects [or don't pick and choose therein]."* - *(42:13)*

(III) THE *DEEN* OF ALL HUMANS

Allah said:

> "*Say (O' Muhammad) Oh Mankind! I am the messenger of Allah to you all."* - *(7:158)*

Messengers before Prophet Muhammad (Peace Be Upon Him) were sent to their people in a specific area and specific time. They addressed their nations and made it clear that they were sent by Allah. Allah said:

> "O my nations worship Allah (alone) there is no any other god for you except him."

This was the call and message of Noah (7:59), the call of Prophet Hud (7:65). Also, it was of Prophet Salih (7:78) and was that of Prophet Shuaib (7:85). Peace Be Upon All of Them.

Prophet Lot, even though he was not originally from of Sodom, was sent to the people there. They were his addressees, so they were called his nation, and he addressed them only

> "And (remember) Lot when he said to his nation...."
> (7:80)

Abraham, the father of the Messengers, also addressed his nation.

Allah said:

> "When he (Abraham) said to his father and his nation, what are these images to which you are devoted." -
> (21:52)

Prophet Moses was sent to Pharaoh and his people, even though he was not from Pharaoh's nation as Pharaoh was Egyptian and Moses was from Bani Israel. Moses was sent for two things

1. To call both nations towards Allah.

2. First, to ask Pharaoh to set Bani Israel free and give them their fundamental rights.

Allah said:

> "Go to Pharaoh; [for] indeed, he has transgressed [the boundaries]." - (20:24, 79:17)

> "So set free with me the children of Israel." - (7:105)

Also, Allah said:

> "Verily Pharaoh exalted himself in the land [of Misr] and divided its people into groups oppressing a group from them, slaughtering their sons and leaving their women alive. Indeed he was from those who were spreading disorder. And we wished to do a favor to those who were oppressed in the land and to make them rulers and to make them the inheritors and to give them the power to show Pharaoh and Haman and their hosts (to receive) from them which they used to fear of." - (28:4-6)

Later on, when Pharaoh was destroyed, then Moses used to address the children of Israel. Allah said:

> "And [remember] when Moses said to his people O my people." - (61:5, 2:54)

JESUS ALSO ADDRESSED TO BANI ISRAEL.

> "O Children of Israel, indeed I am the Messenger of Allah to you." - (61:6)

Their message was one and the same.

Allah said:

> "And we have not sent before you any Messenger but we revealed to him that there is no god except me so worship me (alone)." - (21:25)

These prophets fulfilled their obligation in their respective areas and times. Moreover, when the last and final prophet of Allah, Prophet Muhammad, came, he was sent to the whole world and all human beings, so he addressed them in general as "O Mankind."

Islam is not a religion because "religion" means any system of faith and worship. So, beyond faith, that is a set of a few rituals. While Islam is not a set of a few rituals, it is a complete code and system of life and that is why Allah said:

"Enter into Islam as a whole." - (2:208)

Deen means action, interaction, recompense, submission, domain, system, law, et cetera. Moreover, technically the revealed and divine system given by Allah to the Messengers started with Adam, processed through all the Messengers, and completed with Muhammad. Allah said:

"This day we perfected for you, your Deen *[system] and completed upon you, my favor and chose for you Islam as a* Deen *(system)." - (5:3)*

Allah called it his favor after that he mentioned its completion. This means it will qualify for each and every need of one's people.

Food is a favor when one is hungry; water is a favor when one is thirsty, and so on. Moreover, then he said, "I have chosen it as a system for you, and I am pleased with this for you as a system."

Now Allah is the creator, and he knows all our needs, qualities, and shortcomings. So, he calls a system in his favor, and then for sure it means that the system will be an answer to each and every question and need of ours.

As we have given a pledge of allegiance to Allah, which is the "Kalimah" or the declaration of Islam, "There is no god except Allah and Muhammad is the messenger of Allah." The first part expresses the purpose of our life that it is to believe in Allah as "Ilah" in every field of our life and to obey, practice, and implement his rules and laws.

The second part shows us the way of life and how we will obey, practice, and implement. That must be learned from the "Seerah" (teachings) of Prophet Muhammad. This pledge of allegiance and its details is called "Deen" and Islam,

Allah said:

> *"Verily* Deen *near to Allah is Islam and whoever will seek except Islam anything as* Deen *so it will never be accepted of him, and he is in the hereafter from amongst the losers."*

This verse means that *Deen* is only Islam, and only Islam is *Deen*. Another meaning is that the system close to Allah is Islam only, and it is unacceptable to seek something else as a system.

ALLAH IS THE LAWGIVER

As we said above, the inventor gives users instructions about his invention.

FOR A LAWGIVER IT IS MUST:

1. TO HAVE COMPREHENSIVE KNOWLEDGE NOT ONLY OF THE PRESENT BUT ABOUT THE FUTURE AS WELL.

2. HAS AN IRRESISTIBLE POWER TO HOLD EVERYONE ACCOUNTABLE FOR THEIR ACTIONS.

3. HAS INCLUSIVE MERCY, WHICH INCLUDES EVERYONE EVEN THE ENEMY.

4. TO BE NON-BIASED.

These qualities are the qualities of Allah alone, so only he can give the proper laws to humans. He made the Prophet bound to implement these divine laws.

> "He (Allah) is the one who sent his messenger with guidance and (with), the true "Deen" so he may make it prevail/overcome over all the "Deen" (systems)." - (9:33,48:28,61:9)

In Chapter 9 and Chapter 61 before this verse, Allah mentioned that the enemies of this "Deen" try to extinguish the light of Allah, and by this light, Allah means his "Deen." Allah said:

> *"Allah is the friend of those who believed, brings them out of darkness to light."* - *(2:257)*

Also, He said to his Prophet:

> *"The book we have sent down to you so you may bring the people out of the darkness to light with the leave of their Lord."* - *(14:1)*

Allah ordered the Prophet to judge according to revelation even though the people will try to deviate you from this. Allah said:

> *"And so judge between them by what Allah has revealed and follow not their vein desires and beware of them lest they turn you far away from some of that which Allah has sent down to you?"* - *(5:49)*

Moreover, if there are people who do not want to accept this system and judgment, then Allah said:

> *"So no! by your Lord, they cannot be [perfect] believers until they made you a judge regarding whatever is disputed amongst them and then they don't find any resistance to what you [i.e., your system] have decreed and admit in full."* - *(4:65)*

Here in this verse, it is said, "whatever is disputed" means in each and every field, so this system must be adopted as a package because its different aspects are connected to one another. Allah said:

> *"So will you believe in some parts of the book and will disbelieve in some others, so what is the recompense*

of one who does so from amongst you except humiliation in the life of this world and on the day of resurrection they would be taken to the severe punishment and Allah is not unaware of what you do." - (2:85)

DEEN, SHARIA, AND FIQH

We already discussed the term *Deen*, but what is *Sharia* and what is *Fiqh*? These terms are very common in Islamic sciences.

The word *Sharia* or *Shir'ah* means a broad way that is very clear and open. While Sharia means a known law, this term is used for divine law, so almost everyone assumes it to refer to that. This word is also used synonymously with *Deen*.

Fiqh literally means "to understand" but as a religious term it means the rules and laws of Islam, which is taken from its sources. This term is also used synonymously with both *Deen* and *Sharia*. However, for academic purposes the difference between *Sharia* and *Fiqh* is that *Sharia* means the laws mentioned in the Quran and Sunnah, while *Fiqh* means laws derived from Quran and Sunnah by jurists through analogical deduction.

Thus, *Sharia* is unchangeable while the laws of *Fiqh* can be changed if the situation calls for it. *Sharia* are divine laws given by Allah whose knowledge is comprehensive and He knew that they would always be applicable. Jurists, however, deduce *Fiqh* according to circumstances and situations.

NECESSITY IS AUTHORITY

As we said above, humans are animalistic in nature, ruled by their desires, and they are also social. However, because humans have both desires and intellect, they will use that intellect to fulfill their desires. They will attack others, and thus they need authority to keep them in control and to bring them to justice if they do wrong. Otherwise, turmoil will overtake the whole world and anarchy will prevail.

Unfortunately, human intellect is not a sufficient source of knowledge. It needs illumination, and it cannot illuminate itself, as one thing could never be the cause of the result as well. So, it requires something else far ahead in approach of this intellect, and that is a revelation. Furthermore, intellect and reason have limits beyond which they cannot go further.

While there are things needed and required to be human, those things need another source that can exceed the limits of the intellect and that is revelation. Also, reason and intellect does not know how to fulfill its spiritual needs and, as we know from living in this material world, it needs material things. That even affects the intellect and then its approach will be terrible, and that is why an authority is needed and that authority must be subject to revelation. Otherwise, humans will do the same wrongs as other but will do even worse things as they have desires and authority.

A question arises about whether this authority is mandatory or simply recommended.

There is one group of people called *Faudawiyah* (anarchists) who say all people are equal, so no one may have authority over the others. This is a strange idea and does not make sense. In reality, it is naturally the other way around. Parents have authority over their children, and even these people do not deny nor oppose that. Karl Marx said the same thing, but we say, it is only a hypothesis or a theoretical concept due to its impracticality.

Now there remain only two opinions:

1. AUTHORITY IS PERMISSIBLE BUT NOT A MUST

If people do not want authority than that is neither a sin nor a crime. Often authority brings lots of wrongs and evils. So, if people do not want it, then that is against the concept of natural freedom, equality, and freedom of expression. However, we say that it depends upon whether or not there are corrupt people in authority. We cannot throw away the very concept, but we get rid of corrupt people and then the advantages of having an authority are much greater than the disadvantages. This concept is an extremely negative approach.

2. THE SECOND OPINION IS THAT AUTHORITY AND LEADERSHIP IS ARE MUST AND THEREFORE MANDATORY.

The Prophet of Allah said,

> *"When three people are going on a journey, then they may make one of them their Ameer (leader)"* (Abu Dawud).

It is *Wajib* and must, but for whom? The Imamiyah Shities said this is the duty of Allah and not of the people to appoint an Imam (leader) for the people- this is also the opinion of Ismaili Shities.

These Shities said that an Imam has many advantages and benefits for the public. Also, is a protection and defense from disadvantages and harms. Moreover, this can put people in the right direction to make their lives in both worlds good. However, human beings cannot choose their own Imams as humans have desires, anger, and superstitions, and they cannot differentiate good from bad. So, it is the duty of Allah to give them an Imam to lead, defend, and guide them. To them, the Imam must be a *Masum*, i.e., a person who does not commit any sins. So, they say that an Imam is like a prophet and messenger. He must have the same qualities as a prophet. That is why they say that this is a must for a messenger to express clearly, who is and will be the Imam and he did for Ali and his offspring after him.

The Zaidiyah Shiites said that the prophet mentioned and expressed the required qualities of an Imam. Moreover, these were found in Ali in a perfect manner, so he was the more eligible person to be the Imam. However, Abu Bakr, Umar, and Uthman got it before Ali. This was acceptable but not ideal.

The Imamiyah Shities say, the leadership of these three was wrong, and that was a form of tyranny and oppression and they even say that Abu Bakr, Umar, and Uthman lost their faith.

1. THEY SAID THE PROPHET SAID TO ALI

> *"You are for me like Harun was for Moses."* When Moses was going to Mount Tur (Mount Sinai) he left Harun (Aaron) as his substitute Khalifa and said to him, *"Replace me among my people; act right and follow not the path of those who spread mischief"* (5:142).

2. ZAID IBN ARQAM NARRATED THAT THE PROPHET SAID IN

"Ghadeeri Khum" "o people! Indeed Allah is my Maula, and I am the Maula of the believers and I am prior to them than their selves, so whoever believes I am his Maula than Ali is his Maula, o Allah! Befriend of one who befriended him and be enemy of one who has enmity with him, help the one who helped him, and put down the one who put him down" (Ahmad, Hakim, Nisa'i, Tabrani).

3. THE PROPHET GAVE HIM A FLAG IN THE BATTLE OF KHAYBAR.

He had said,

"Tomorrow I will give the flag to one who loves Allah and his Messenger and Allah and his Messenger love him, and he turns to the enemy and does not run away; he will not come back when Allah gives victory to his hand." (Bukhari, Tirmizi, Hakim)

4. They said there is a Hadith that

   "Ali is the best judgment giver"

So, it means he is eligible for *Khalafah*.

5. They say:

a) That the knowledge of humans is not sufficient to appoint an Imam as the Imam may be a *Masum*, so only a *Masum* may appoint him.

b) Also, a Khalifa is the representative of Allah and his messenger and not that of the people, so how can people choose the representative of Allah and his Messenger?

c) If this is left to the people, then there will be disputes, differences, enmity, hatred, and bloodshed, which is against the very wisdom of "Khalafah" as the role of a Khalifa is to maintain peace.

However, we say that the Prophet left Ali behind when he was going to the expedition of "Tabuk." So, the hypocrites said that the Prophet does not like him, and he left him behind. Ali came to the Prophet and was crying that he was leaving Ali amongst the women and children; then the Prophet said, " You don't want to be my Khalifa as Harun was to Moses." So, this cannot be a base for his Khalafah, as the Prophet used to leave behind different people as his representative on different occasions.

In the Hadith of "Ghadeeri-Khum", Allama Eiji said (in his book *Al Mawaqif*) that this Hadith is not authentic, as Ali was in Yemen at that time. He was not with the Prophet in "Ghadeeri Khum" and those who narrated this do not mentioned the background how and why the Prophet said it. Moreover, even if it is proven still, it does not mean that he is Khalifa; the word *Maula* has many meanings, such as helper, protector, friend, master, emancipated slave, cousin, shelter, ally, et cetera.

So, which one is meant here? Also, Imam Abu Dawud and Abu Hatim Ar-Razi have reservations about the authenticity of this Hadith. Also, the Prophet said regarding Juhaimah Muzainah, Aslam and Ghifar tribes that they are my *Mawali* (plural of *Maula*), so does it mean they will be the rulers after the Prophet?

Regarding the Hadith of Khaybar that Allah and his Messenger love him, it does not mean that he is Khalifa, because Allah said:

"Then soon Allah will bring a people he will love them and they will love him, humble towards the believers, stern towards the disbelievers, fighting in the way of Allah having no fear of the blame of those who blame." - (5:54)

So, does it mean that all these people will be *Khulafa*?

The Hadith, which says that "Ali is the best judgment giver", doesn't mean eligibility for *Khalafah*. Because in the same Hadith the Prophet said before that "the kindest towards my Ummah is Abu Bakr, the strong one in the *Amar* (*Deen*/rule) of Allah is Umar, the most truthful in decency is Uthman..." Then kindness is another quality making one eligible, and strength in the rule of Allah is another eligibility, and decency another, as well as that of judgment. Moreover, the Prophet said it in the sequence in which the Khalafah was passed down.

As for disputes, we say that things could never be dropped because of "ifs" and "buts." Sharia made it clear who deserves to be the *Khalifa* and who will choose him. Their qualities and requirements are clearly stated and being the Khalifa means being the viceroy of Allah to implement his "Deen" over the people and the actual *Khalafah* of Allah is with the people.

The 2nd opinion is that of Ahlus - Sunnah that *Khalafah* is *Wajib* (a must) based on the Quran, the Sunnah, the Ijma, and reason as well.

1. The Holy Quran says:

   "O you who believe! Obey Allah and obey the messenger and the people in authority."

It means that there may be people in authority, and their obedience is a must if they are from amongst you, meaning they are not a colonial power, nor may they order against the Quran and Sunnah. There should be no obedience to the creation that would result in disobedience to the Creator.

2. There are several Ahadith in this regard even the *Muhaditheen* have written chapters in this regard.

The Prophet said:

> *"Leadership is must and people cannot avoid leaders" (Abu Dawud). Meaning that they have to have leaders and leadership. The Prophet of Allah also said: An Imam (leader) is a shield" (Bukhari, Muslim).*

3. This is based on the *Ijma* (consensus) of Sahaba after the death of the Prophet. Even the delayed burial of the Prophet until a Khalifa could be chosen shows the importance of this issue in Sharia. That is why they gathered together on the porch of Banu Sa'idah. There was a lengthy process and discussion when Umar said of Abu Bakr that the Prophet chose him for leadership in *Deen*. Which means to lead the prayer, so shouldn't we choose him for the leadership of our worldly affairs? Moreover, then unanimously they chose Abu Bakr and gave their pledge of allegiance to him, because of the importance of *Ijma*. Abu Bakr nominated Umar in his last moments. Umar appointed a *Shura* (consultative council) to choose a Khalifa, about which we will give the details later, Insha'Allah (Allah willing).

4. The world needs peace. There is no peace but with justice, and justice is to be administered by an authority that can implement it, as Allah said:

> *"Indeed Allah orders justice and kindness." - (16:9)*

> *"Do justice that is very nearer to piety." - (5:8)*

If justice is not there then of course there will be disorder and mischief. Allah said:

> *"And seek not mischief in the land; verily Allah does not like those who spread mischief/disorder." - (28:77)*
>
> *"And Allah does not like mischief." - (2:205)*

Imam Ghazali, the great thinker, said,

> *That each has two basic duties: knowledge and worship. Both depend upon health, safety, and the availability of needs and necessities (Al Iqtisad fil I'tiqad).*

Ensuring the safety and availability of requirements is not possible without a system, and that is why some Muslim scholars have defined politics as: *"Correction of the life in this world and the life in the hereafter."* When someone is safe and satisfied in his life, he can worship Allah to the best of his ability.

Imam Nasafi has written that an Imam is a must for Muslims to implement the rules of Allah, control those who do wrong, resolve conflicts, arrange defense, and collect the taxes, and charities (Al Aqa'id).

The Imam of sociology and politics, Imam Al Mawardi, mentions a similar thing, that this is a must for an authority structure capable of defending the *Deen* and the state, controlling criminals, and maintaining law and order (*Adabud Deen Wad Dunya*). Allama Al Eiji in "Al Mawaqif" and "Al Aamidi in "Abkarul Afkar" have both said this as well.

So according to Sunni scholars, Khalafah is a must, and the duty of choosing a Khalifa falls to the Ummah, who must possess the required qualities, based not on intellect but rather on Islamic order and commandments while according to Mutazilite and Shiites this must be based on intellect and reason. Hasan Al Basri and some other scholars say it is based on both.

We say this is a *Wajibi Shar'ee* supported by reason and intellect, because Islam does not suspend the human intellect but specifies its field and puts it behind Sharia. It does not allow it to go ahead of Sharia or to exceed and overrule Sharia. Allah said:

> "O you who believe, don't go ahead of Allah and his messenger and fear Allah verily Allah is all hearing, all knowing." - (49:1)

Islam has given a principle in every field, and still it has left a vast field for intellect but with a condition. Its application may be by the rules laid down by the authentic scholars of Quran and Sunnah. These rules are derived from the Quran and Sunnah, about which Allah said:

> "Then ask the people of Zikr *(expertise) if you do not understand."* - (21:7)

The fourth source of Islamic Sharia, which is *Qiyas* or analogical deduction, is the intellectual approach of a jurist having sufficient knowledge of Quran and Sunnah.

KHALAFAH

Before discussing this term's meaning we want to talk about another term of the modern world for the stated purpose of rule and government they use, and that is "politics."

"Politic" has more than one meaning such as prudent, wise, shrewd, advisable, cunning. These words are used for a person having these qualities, although some of these qualities are good while some others, like cunning, are not good.

"Politics" means the art of government and political affairs, but as a subject of study, it is called political science.

"Politician" means a member of a political party, a statesman, a holder of a political position. Anyone who is dealing diplomatically is called someone who is cunning or the one who does not disclose him or the matters very much. In English, there is another word, "polite," which is spelled nearly the same and means a refined and polished person. So, a politician should be refined and polished. A statesman is one who puts his or her constituents and their interests ahead of his or her own aims.

Nowadays Arab-speaking people use the word *As-Siyasah* as a substitute for politics or political science. Hafiz Ibn Taymiyyah has a book on this topic by the name of *As-Siyastush-Sharia*. *Siyasah* means "taking the responsibility of a thing to fix it." So, for fixing cities, states, and governments we can use the word *As-Siyasatul-Madania* to mean the *Siyasah* of societies, cities, and states and the people that live therein. So then *As-Siyasah* or politics means responsibility of society, state, or government to fix society. It means reformation, correction and striving for perfection, even though perfection is nowhere in the world, and that is always room for further improvements.

Improvements can be made in both developed countries and developing countries until the last day. That is why the world is called "Hadith" ephemeral as it came into existence from no existence. Changes are taking place throughout time, and there will be no perfection in this world. More work and striving hard for it will be needed. This will be going on until the big crunch causes the world to disappear. The only perfect entity is Allah, and the only perfect human being is the Prophet Muhammad. That is why he was sent as the final Prophet until the Day of Judgment. We can say that the system is given by that perfect entity Allah, to the perfect human being Muhammad. It is for guidance for the whole word until the last day. It is the only perfect system for humans in general, even for those who do not believe in him and his message.

Here is what a non-Muslim said about Islam. George Bernard Shaw, a philosopher, thinker, and writer, wrote that if the whole world became only one state having different caste, colors, cultures, languages, and even religions, it would need a system that can protect people and their rights and in which everyone can live in peace with one another. That system can only be the one given by Muhammad.

However, in Islamic Sharia the term used for this is *Khalafah*. Sometimes scholars use the term *Imamah* or *Imarah*. These terms are also used in the sayings of the Prophet or his companions. However, it is unfortunate that *Khalafah* is not properly understood in the non-Muslim world, because either they have learned about some Muslim rulers or heard about them doing wrong practices that have nothing to do with Islam but rather local culture or they think that *Khalafah* means to make all other religions perish. This misconception makes Islam seem brutal and discriminatory, which is totally wrong. The history of Muslims is sufficient evidence of this: Muslims ruled both India and Spain for almost 1000 years each, but today neither is a Muslim majority country. This means the leaders never forced or oppressed them to convert to Islam. Allah said:

"There is no compulsion in Deen *[religion] - (2:256)*

The Medina treaty is also ample proof that the Prophet of Allah provided surety to the non-Muslims in the city of Medina. The treaty expressed the respect for their rights on an equal basis (see our book "Islam the Misunderstood Religion in the West").

The *Khalifa* was the successor of the Prophet. This title was used for Abu Bakr in reality, as he was the direct successor of the Prophet. After him, the second successor said, *"Khalifa* of Abu Bakr the *Khalifa* of the Prophet, as Abu Bakr was after the Prophet. However, I am after Abu Bakr so the case will be the *Khalifa* of the *Khalifa*, and it will keep prolonging later. So, you should call me *'Amirul Momineen,' the leader of the believers."* However, this term *Khalifa* later became the title of the Muslim rulers. They said that every Muslim and ruler is the *Khalifa* of Allah in the meaning of his agent, or he is the *Khalifa* of the Prophet in the system given by the Prophet. That is why Muslim scholars adopted this word for their discussion and their writings as well, while others adopted the term "Al-Ahkam As Sultania" as they are of the view that the word *Khalafah* is not that important. The scholars defined "Khalafah" in different ways, but the meaning is almost the same.

1. Allama Abul Hasan Al Mawardi defined "Al Imamah" as the succession of the prophethood in guarding the *Deen* and in the politics of the world (*Al-Ahkam Al Sultania*).

Analysis:

    a) *Imamat* is the succession of prophethood.

    b) The purpose of *Imamat* is to guard the *Deen*.

    c) Moreover, to plan of the affairs of this world.

    d) When it is the succession of the prophethood, so it is not the personal right of an individual (i.e., the Khalifa and the Imam) but that is the right of the followers of the Prophet (i.e., the *Ummah*). So, they have to choose someone for this, and the person chosen is bound to take care of these two things:

i. Guarding *Deen*.

ii. Planning for this world.

    2. Allama Iddud Din Al-Eiji said:

"Succession of the Messenger in implementation of Deen and in the protection of Millat (nation) in a way that the entire ummah is bound to follow." (Al-Mawaqif)

Analysis:

a) *Khalafah* is the succession of the messenger of Allah.

b) Its responsibility is to keep the *Millat* united.

c) It will implement *Deen*.

d) The whole *ummah* is bound to obey and to follow this authority; again, this definition made it clear that it is the right and duty of the *Ummah*. Also, the definition excluded the authority of the judge and jurist as that is binding on the parties concerned and that his responsibility is not general and inclusive.

3. Imam Fakhrud din Razi said:

   "General authority for someone from amongst them in Deen and worldly affairs as a succession from the Prophet" - *(Nihayatul Uqul)*

Analysis:

a) This is the succession of the Messenger.

b) This is a general authority, so it excluded the judge and jurist, as theirs is a special authority.

c) The authority is in both *Deen* and worldly affairs.

d) This belongs genuinely to the *ummah*, but they must choose one of them for the said responsibility. That one must have the required qualities, and then taking care of Deen and worldly affairs is his responsibility.

4. Allama Taftazani said:

   "General authority in the affairs of Deen and worldly life as a succession from the Prophet" - *(Sharhul Aqa'id)*

This definition is very similar to that of Imam Razi. However, Taftazani does not mention "for someone from amongst them" but that is understood as the whole *Ummah*, or a group of people cannot be the *Khalifa;* only one person that is eligible.

5. Allama Saifud Din Al-Aamidi mentioned in Abkarul Afkar,

> "Succession of the Messenger is for a person from amongst them in implementing the laws of Sharia and protection of the Millat in a way that the whole Ummah may obey and follow."

Analysis:

a) This is the Succession of the Messenger.

b) To keep the *ummah* united and to implement the rule of Islamic Sharia.

c) The entire *Ummah* is its source, but it may be given to one from among them.

d) The entire *ummah* is bound to obey and to follow.

This is a more inclusive definition, but the well-known scholar, philosopher, and thinker Ibn Khaldun said,

> "To put all of their Islamic thoughts regarding their good in the hereafter and they are good here which eventually go towards the hereafter."

So, to him the *Khalafah* is

> "Succession of the bearer of Sharia in guarding of Deen *and planning of this world based on it (*Deen*).*"

In brief, all these definitions mean the good of the Hereafter and this world based on *Deen*. That becomes possible when *Deen* is followed in each walk of life, and that is only possible when there will be an authority guarding *Deen* and implementing that why here two things become clear:

1. *Deen* is not a personal thing for an individual, but everyone must push each other in *Deen* and especially the authority, as Allah said:

   "Those whom we give them power in the land they establish (system of) prayer and give Zakat [almsgiving] and they enjoin good and forbid evil and to Allah return the result of all affairs." - (22:41)

2. *Deen* does not only deal with the individual affairs but with social, economic, political, national, and international as well. Moreover, that is why Allah called it *Deen* and ordered to enter it as a whole.

Allah said:

"Verily Deen *near Allah is Islam [only]." - (3:19)*

"And whoever seeks besides Islam any Deen *will never be accepted, and he will be of the losers" (3:85).*

Moreover, Allah said:

"O you who believe! Enter into Islam as a whole (totally) and do not follow the footsteps of Satan; verily he is for you an obvious enemy" (2:208)

This is not like secularism to take *Deen* out of worldly life totally and think that *Deen* has nothing to do with public life and that *Deen* is the personal business of everyone. This theory destroys the concept of accountability. Because if someone has the fear of Allah and the fear of the Day of Judgment, that fear will make him in line with the *Deen* in every field or capacity. Then that person will never violate any rule or anyone's rights.

TYPES OF GOVERNMENTS

Governments in the modern world are of two kinds:

1) DICTATORIAL GOVERNMENT

The government of a person with absolute power, or an autocratic government. In this sort of government, the person in power forces others to follow and obey his commands and no one may oppose him.

2) DEMOCRATIC GOVERNMENT

That is a government of elected people. The people elect their representatives or their leadership in the institutions, usually by a simple majority. In other words, it is a form of government for the people by the will of the majority of the people (based on the concept of equality).

In the first type, the dictator runs the state based on his desires while in the second type the state is run based on the desires of the elected people and their majority. Desires are desires, whether that is of an individual or a group based on the majority. Even though there is a constitution, which is the fundamental law, there is a very wide range of desires and many loopholes. The public elect this group and they hand themselves over to that group for four or five years to decide their destiny. In such a system the spiritual side of humans, their moral side, and their life in the hereafter, is not considered at all. Rather, is ignored and considered against the concept of democracy and specifically of secularism and secular democracy. Also, when this is clubbed together with capitalism, then it becomes harmful, as capitalism looks at material gains and benefits only and then make it decisions.

So, let us see in brief, what is Secularism and how was it introduced?

SECULARISM

After Jesus, Christianity was perverted to such an extent that this religion of monotheism changed to a religion of polytheism. Moreover, a creature is not only considered an associate of God but a part of God or even God and Lord. For sins, one must repent to Allah, but in a perverted concept he has to pay his expiation and atonement to the religious leader and the religious leader will pardon him. The greatness of humans is their socialization, but in this perverted shape of religion one must go to seclusion and retreat and withdraw from people to get close to God.

These concepts are against human nature and against the very spirit of a divine religion. On the other hand, the kingship became tyrannical, and the church had nothing to do with the worldly affairs. Also, scientific research or new theories based upon research were considered an apostasy by the Church. They gave religious verdicts against that and to get a decree from the king to hang or burn that scholar, scientist, or researcher. They killed thousands of people to stop and discourage new discoveries, research, and developments. They put in the minds of the kings that their discoveries are not only against religion but also a threat to the kingship and its majesty.

In such a situation, the state used to give grants to the church and the church would not say anything regarding the kings and whatever they were doing. It means that the religious people were a shield for the kings and their wrongdoings and cruelty. Also, the religious people were considered holy, and nobody could say a single word against them for fear of severe punishment. This started in 486 A.D. and was at its peak in 540-640 A.D. at the time of Pope Gregory I; this holiness was called a theocracy. So, it continued until the 18th century.

The concept of church and religion created many skeptics and rejecters. These rejecters of religion started in the Middle Ages and some movements in the name of Liberalism, Humanism, and Rationalism began. When these movements stepped into the political field, then the secular democracy was introduced, which means a government for the people by the will of most of the people.

Now when we say democracy, then that is a culture, and you must take it with the secular concept. Also, when secularism, democracy, and material science are clubbed together, then the criteria will be what are good for the people in their material world. Legislation must follow that and to comply with it, as religion or ethics may not be given any room or any preference over that. Material science does not discuss immaterial things, something that an ordinary human does not sense. Nor you can take it to a lab to test whether it is important.

Furthermore, let us see when secularism not as a philosophy but rather a system was introduced? The founder of this type of thinking was George Holyoake; he was born in 1817 in Birmingham, England. His parents were artists although he grew up in a religious atmosphere. However, in 1832 when the bill for reforms came forward, he decided to withdraw from the church and get in touch with some social missionaries.

However, in 1841 he fell into agnosticism and was imprisoned for blasphemous remarks against God. He wrote in his newspaper clearly that we are not infidels if infidelity means to reject Christian beliefs, as he did not reject it, merely criticized its wrong concepts and wrongdoings. He was not affiliated in any way with atheists but the contradictions in Christianity pushed him to declare that religion is not that important. He died in 1906. His colleague Thomas Cooper also became reactionary; he established the principles of the Chartism Movement. In 1856, he was imprisoned for two years when a Christian leader rejected his political enthusiasm. He wrote some papers in Christianity's defense, but he was active for a non-religious society even though later he came back to the fold of Christianity.

When we investigate the work of their two basic thinkers of secularism, we know that Holyoake separated secularism from atheism. "Secular" is derived from the Latin *seculam*, which means "this present age." However, nowadays two terms are very suitable for those who write

(I) "MATERIALISM" AND

(II) SECULARISM

So, they have drawn a line in between religion and politics because the political field is non-religious. Rousseau, Haneke, and others made it even more scientific; it's very founders gave a philosophical concept. That had a specific relation to morality but later its productivity in the political field gave it a non-religious interpretation. In the last half of the 20th century, some religious people tried to introduce secular Christianity to pull Christianity into politics. They said that Christianity qualifies our needs in every field. But as the church's concepts practiced in the past had introduced a different picture of Christianity that it supports wrong doings of the authority, protects feudalism, and tries to stop research, science, new discoveries, and invention.

So, the Western world did not take to this concept of secular Christianity, and they said religious interference in social and political life is fundamentalism. Fundamentalism was a defamed term used at the time when the church said that humans by nature are evil. Moreover, he or she will do that evil action, and that evil requires punishment, but Allah is merciful and doesn't have any interest in punishing people. However, there should be some way out, so he sent his son Jesus who was crucified. Moreover, that crucifixion is an expiation for the sins of all those who believe in him as a savior. So, his representatives in the church can pardon people, and their sins get washed away.

Peter Waldo Vaux, John Toler, John Luther, and others started this concept of practicing Christianity in every field of life. They protested the church and its wrongdoings and making religion an easy way of earning. They spoke against the church and wanted to bring actual Christianity back and implement it into daily life in every way, including social and political life. These people were called Protestants. The Church supported and protected the wrongdoings of the authority and kings. The Church opposed science, knowledge, and research. Fundamentalism was defined as "interference of religion in social, political, and economical life" or the rule of religion.

Moreover, keeping in view this historical background of this term, when this term will be said regarding any religion, the public will buy it, and that's why nowadays this term is used very frequently Anyhow, secularism came into existence to counter this concept and movement. It is defined as "ethical doctrine that advocates a moral code independent of all religious considerations or practices or the view or belief that societies values and standards should not be influenced by religion and church". Moreover, when religion and science are considered opposite to one another then secularism got fame and acceptance because people are influenced by science because they see its benefits, so how can they reject it. So, they accepted secularism and that religion have nothing to do with the public atmosphere and that it is a personal thing for everyone.

Secular people say that if religion interferes in a state, then it minimizes the field of legislation. This is not right because Islam in its texts has given the principles. However, it has given a vast field to human intellect to make and frame laws for the good of humans and society. However, it has neither straightened the situation nor has it entirely suspended human reason. Nor has it given unbridled power to the intellect, it has bound it to the basic concept and principles of *Deen* (religion).

HOW AND WHY WAS SECULARISM INTRODUCED AND ADOPTED?

Humans by nature do not like many restrictions. They do not like oppression but rather oppose it. Evils are disliked by them by nature, but as we said that evils prevailed and.

I. Instead of stopping and opposing it to protect, defend, and pardon, religion introduced the concept that humans by nature are drawn to evil. Secularism was a reaction to that wrong concept of religion, which is why it was accepted.

II. The selfishness of the feudalist, influential and rich people provided access to secularism. These people used the religion by giving financial support to the church, and the church defended them.

III. The Church was not expressing human nature but rather it was oppressing it, and that was unnatural.

IV. The Church used to oppose the research, knowledge, science, and developments.

V. The Church was opposing any religious or political freedom to an irrational level.

This caused an untenable situation, and it came in the shape of secularism and suchlike situations the people accept with excitement. So, secularism was not only an ideology but also a reaction to religion as well. Such a thing that comes into existence as a reaction has both pros and cons. The after-effects of reactionary emotions, negation of the recognized facts, and limited approach were some of these. Now keeping in view, the background, we say that those who said that Islam is equal to secularism plus God is wrong because plus means affirmation. However, in secularism God is not the subject either to believe or disbelieve. Yes, Horway said that a secular person is a man of this modern age while a religious one is an Orthodox person, but secularism has its roots in the Bible, so this is not against religion.

So, secularism turned out religious aspect from the social, economic, and political fields and confined it to a few beliefs and a few rituals and disseminated the notion that religion is everyone's personal business.

Then after this philosophy, all modern systems were established based on this. Western capitalism is based on three pillars: humanism, rationalism, and materialism, but the Industrial Revolution divided the humans into two categories: industrialists and workers. Capital is the base and actual axis while human being is a part of the industry, and what results from this is exploitation. As a reaction socialism and communism were introduced and as we know that sometimes the reaction is worse than the action and can be more virulent. The base was the same, secularism, but it shaped to an even worse form, which is secular capitalism, which does not discuss God and religion positively nor negatively but rather it considers it illegal, and in communism they negate God and religion as a whole.

ISLAMIC SYSTEM OF GOVERNMENT

In this system the government is based on Quran and Sunnah, where all people are equal regardless of their caste, color, sect, or religion, and where the people in authority are the agents of God and the servants of the public. This type of government is bound to provide needs and necessities to all without discrimination and to establish justice and peace.

IMAM ABU DAWUD NARRATED FROM ADI THAT

The prophet of Allah told me, O Adi! When Islam will prevail, you will see a pretty woman with lots of wealth travelling alone from Basrah (Iraq) to Makah (Saudi Arabia) without no fear of any attack, and O Adi! When Islam prevails, you will see the treasury of the Romans and Persians under the feet of the Muslims and O Adi! When Islam will prevail, you will see that in a big gathering someone will offer a bag full of wealth as Zakat if someone is eligible for it, but there will be no one ready to take it. Adi said, I saw the first thing in the time of Umar, and the second thing in the time of Uthman when the treasury of Hurmuzan was there in the open field outside the masjid (mosque) of the Prophet and the third one he said to his students, maybe you will see it later.

Moreover, that occurred in the time of Umar Ibn Abdul Aziz Umawi, who was a pious and God-fearing ruler. Once in a gathering nobody was there in the gathering of thousands ready to accept *Zakat* (alms giving), as everyone's needs and necessities were fulfilled and they were self-sufficient.

THE SOURCES OF ISLAMIC LAW

There are two types of sources for Islamic law:

(I) FUNDAMENTAL SOURCES

These sources are four in number:

    a.   The Holy Quran.

    b.   The Sunnah (teachings) of the Prophet of Allah.

    c.   *Ijma* or consensus of opinions of the jurists of the ummah.

    d.   *Qiyas* or analogical deduction or analogy.

Qiyas means to examine, approximate or to measure while technically it means comparing *Furoo*, a sub-division of Islamic law, to *Asl*, a situation that ruling is in the text of Quran or Sunnah, because of a common cause.

In *Qiyas*, it is important to determine the operative or effective cause of a known ruling because the rule exists if the operative cause exists. The operative cause is called *illati Jami'a* or *illati Mushtarakah*, which means that Islam has not made all things black and white, but rather it gave principles and rules for further expansion and application. It means Islam has not capped things but left scope for thinking.

(II) SECONDARY SOURCES:

From these sources there a few as listed below:

1. *Urf* or customs, usages, and conventions. When the Prophet was sent, he classified the customs of Arabia into three categories as they were his first addressees:

    I. Totally bad and evil customs like idol worship or the burial of live newborn girls. The Prophet nullified these from day one and said the first is wrong to Allah and the second is wrong towards humanity.

    II. Good customs, like that of giving one hundred camels to the family of the victim of an accidental murder, so the Prophet kept it as is.

    III. A custom partially good and partially bad, like marriage.

The Quraish used force women and girls into marriage and there was no recourse for the family of the girl when a strong or wealthy man put his hand on a girl. Also, they took as many wives as they wished and inherited widows from brothers, uncles, nephews, or cousins.

The Prophet reformed the custom of marriage. He established that women are also human beings that have reason, intellect, and equal to men. Her consent is a must for marriage, to be approved by her guardian for her further respect and dignity. Then she had her due rights in the light of Quran and Sunnah. Also, the Holy Quran limited the maximum number of wives to four but stipulated that a man could only take as many wives up to that limit as he could provide for equally. Otherwise, he would suffer for that injustice in the hereafter. Also, the Prophet of Allah said that there must be two witnesses at the time of the marriage to bear witness this contract to further dignify it. Moreover, there must be a gift to the bride as a mark of respect and a gift. Finally, Allah and his messenger said the husband must provide a residence that he can afford and provide his wife or wives with the needs and necessities according to his means and must not be cruel to her or them. So, these were the reforms towards this practice and custom. So, any custom that does not go against Sharia is not only permissible but based on it laws could be framed.

2. *Istihsan* or preference to a *Qiyas* that is ambiguous while Qiyas is more evident. Because the people do a practice that is ok to the first one but not to the later type of *Qiyas*. So that is legalized because of their pre-involvement in that, or because of their needs and necessities. This is according to Imam Abu Hanifa.

3. *Istislah* or public interest. This means to make a law for the benefit of the public that does not violate the fundamental principles of Islam. This is according to Imam Malik.

This shows that Islam has left a vast field of legislation to the human reason also. Issues arise and need solutions all the time, so if there is no expressed solution, then it is logical to find a solution for it. That is also required by the finality of the prophethood of the Prophet Muhammad.

THE SOURCE OF KHILAFAH

By the source of *Khalafah*, we mean who has the right to give this responsibility to someone? The kingship, lordship, and rule belong to Allah,

As Allah said:

> "Rule is but for Allah." - (6:57/12:40 and 67)

> "Behold! to him [Allah] is the rule." - (6:62)

> "Surely his is the creation and the rule, blessed be Allah, the Lord of the worlds." - (7:45)

> "And He [Allah] makes none share in his rule." - (18:26)

> "And in whatever you differ, the decision thereof is with Allah." - (42:10)

There are dozens of verses that say that Allah is the Lord, the King, and the Ruler, this is but a matter of faith as Allah said:

> "And whosoever does not judge on what Allah has sent down then such like people are the disbelievers." - (5:44)

There is a belief, and then there is practice. If a Muslim does not believe in the rule of Allah, then he is a disbeliever. If he believes in it but does not implement the rule of Allah even though he has the power and the authority, then he is a wrongdoer and a rebel against the command of Allah. Allah said:

> *"And whoever doesn't judge on what Allah has sent down, then such like people are the wrongdoers." - (5:45)*

> *"... Then such like people are rebellious." - (5:47)*

So, from an Islamic perspective, all types of supremacy and sovereignty go to Allah. In the world and throughout its history we see that this supremacy goes to a person who is called either a king or a dictator. In the present world the popular notion is a democracy, which means the supremacy goes to the public. However, if the elected people are not subject to a supreme and sovereign entity, then again, the trend will go towards the particular group or class dictatorship and aristocracy. Here we see if that aristocracy is hereditary (which is usually is) then at least that is a traditionally upper privileged class, and the supremacy goes to that class.

Islam does not believe either in the supremacy of the privileged class nor that of the public. However, rather in the supremacy of Allah alone and that is what the *Kalimah*, or declaration of Islam says

> *"There is no god but Allah, and Muhammad is the messenger of Allah."*

This pledge of allegiance means that humans are subject to Allah in the ways shown by the Prophet Muhammad. Neither an individual is a source of law, nor the general public, and neither a specific class of people but only Allah. Yes, Allah has given the right to the *ummah* to appoint their *Khalifa*, who must have the required qualities and who may be the agent of Allah to apply and implement his rules, and who may be the servant of the public.

Allah said to the Prophet:

> "You are not a dictator over them." - (88:22)

> " You are not the one to compel them by force." - (50:45)

Moreover, Umar, the second successor of the Prophet said when addressing the public.

> "I swear by Allah, I am not a king to enslave you through kingship or by force, I am not but one like you, my position towards you is like the guardian of an orphan towards him and his belongings."

In Islam the *ummah* must appoint their ruler according to the revealed and divine Sharia. That is why the in Islam the divine Sharia, along with the *ummah*, is considered the source of the rule. Which means that source of law is Sharia and source of practice are the *ummahs*. So, the *ummah* appoints the ruler, then they obey him and advise him whenever it is needed, and they impeach him when it is required. Almost all four schools of jurisprudence mention these rights of the *Ummah*, as Ibn Khaldun referred to in *Al Muqaddimah*, Al Mawardi in *Al-Ahkamus Sultania*, Al Baqilani in *At-Tamheed*, and Shah Wali Ullah in *Hujjatullahil Balighah*.

HOW TO APPOINT AND DETERMINE SOMEONE FOR KHALAFAH?

Islam and Islamic history have not mentioned one specific way for this procedure, in this regard the practice in the time of Sahaba as they were the *Khulafa* (successors) and *Khalafah* started with them is the source. So let us investigate the history.

As we said, *Khalafah* and *Khalifa* are a must to rule the affairs of the state as a vacuum brings unsolvable problems. Moreover, that is why right after the death of the Prophet, the *Ansar* (natural inhabitants of Medina) gathered on the porch of Banu Sa'idah to choose a *Khalifa*. They were of the view that the Messenger of Allah was the messenger, and he was our ruler as well, but now, as he is not there anymore. Then we the natural inhabitants have the right to be the *Khalifa*, and they wanted Sa'd Ibn Obadah, Sa'd the chief of the Khazraj tribe, to become the *Khalifa*. Some *Muhajireen* (immigrants) were also present. When Umar heard about the meeting, he took Abu Bakr with him and came to the porch. Abu Bakr told them that the Prophet said that the *Ameers* after him would be from Quraish, so they sat down and became quiet. Then Umar gave his *Bai'at*, or pledge of allegiance, by placing his hand in the hand of Abu Bakr. Moreover, he said that the Prophet had chosen him for our leading in *Deen* (prayers), so can we not choose him for our leadership in worldly affairs? After Umar pledge allegiance, many other people followed him and gave their pledge as well including those *Ansar* (Imam Nawawi narrated similar narration from Ali as well). Before this utterance by Abu Bakr and referring to the Prophet, the situation became so tense that it was close to a fight. Moreover, a suggestion was given that there may be one Ameer from the *Ansar* and one from the *Muhajireen*. So basically, those who were there gave their pledge right there and then and later on the general public gave their pledge on the second day in the masjid. The public realized that those who were considered "Ahlul Halli Wal Aqd" chose Abu Bakr. We will talk about them and their qualities *Insha'Allah*.

When Abu Bakr was in last days, he had experienced the dispute on who was going to become the *Khalifa* after the Prophet, so he decided to choose one from amongst the major Sahaba. He wanted Umar or Ali to become the *Khalifa*, but later he was inspired to choose Umar, whom he thought was the best choice. Abu Bakr was asking everyone that came to inquire about his health about Umar. He asked Abdur Rahman Ibn Auf, and he said, "by Allah he is the best choice but he a little hard." Abu Bakr said, "he was hard because I was very soft." Uthman said, "you know him better than us." Ali said, "his inner self is much better than his outer and nobody is like him." Osaid Ibn Hudam said the same thing about Umar as Ali had. Saeed Ibn Zaid and others also praised Umar and spoke very highly of him. Then Abu Bakr asked Uthman to write the document that said:

In the name of Allah, the Beneficent, the Merciful. This is what Abu Bakr the Khalifa of the Messenger of Allah promised with at the time of his departing from this world and entering the other one. Also, in a situation where the disbeliever is becoming a believer and a wicked one fears, verily I have appointed Umar the son of Khattab so if he does kindness and justice. So that is what I know of him, and that is my opinion of him. However, if he did injustice and changed so I do not have any knowledge of *Ghaib* (things unknown/unseen) and the best I have intended and for everyone is what he has done.

> *"And soon the unjust will come to know which side they are going to turn [or lying down/folding down]."*
> *- (26:227)*

So, Umar became the Khalifa as Abu Bakr appointed him, and the people consented to that. When Abu Lulu hit Umar at dawn prayer and was seriously injured, the Sahaba asked him if he could appoint someone? Umar said whom shall I appoint? If Abu Ubaidah were alive, I would have appointed him and when Allah would have asked me, I would have said that your messenger said, "Abu Ubaidah is the trustee of the *ummah*. Moreover, if Saalim the liberated slave of Abu Huzaifah had been alive, I would have appointed him. And if Allah had asked me, I would have said that your Messenger said that Saalim is in a great love with Allah (in some narrations it is mentioned that he was a man who loves Allah and Allah loves him)." One of them said, "let me show you a person who is eligible if you would appoint him." Umar said, "whom?" The man said, "Abdullah Ibn Umar (son of Umar)." Umar said, "May Allah punish you! We have nothing to do with your affairs. It is enough for the family of Umar that only one man is put to accountability for this duty. I strove hard and deprived my family and if I escape from this accountability having no reward for it and having no sin also, then for sure I am a lucky person". Then he said *"If I would have appointed someone the indeed one who was better then I [Abu Bakr] he had done it and if I did not, then the one who was better than me (Prophet of Allah) had not done it"*- which means both ways we have the procedure of choosing a *Khalifa*.

Once again, the Sahaba came to him asking to appoint someone but he said, "I am leaving this to that group whom from the Messenger of Allah was happy when he was leaving this world and said they are from the people of paradise. They are Uthman, Ali, Sad Ibn Abi Waqas, Abdur Rahman Ibn Auf, Zubair Ibn Awwam, Talha Ibn Ubaid Ullah and with them Abdullah Ibn Umar, but he will not be a candidate for *Khalafah*." So, the *Khalafah* will be from the six Sahaba mentioned above, but if there is a tie in the vote, then the vote of Abdullah Ibn Umar will be the decisive vote. If they did not agree to it, then they should be with the group of Abdur Rahman Ibn Auf. Then Umar ordered Suhaib to lead the prayers after his death. And ordered Uthman, Ali, Zubair, Sa'd, Abdur Rahman, and Talha if he arrived (as he was outside Medina) and brought with Ibn Umar with them to figure out who should be the next *Khalifa*. They were told to choose a *Khalifa* before the fourth day of his death.

Then Abdur Rahman pleaded with them not to consider him for this responsibility, and they agreed, and then they gave the authority to Abdur Rahman to help complete the process. So, he asked Ali, "if he is not chosen then who should be the *Khalifa*?" Ali said Uthman, and then he asked everyone separately so each one except for Uthman, wanted Uthman to be the *Khalifa* while Uthman wanted Ali to be the *Khalifa*. Also, Abdur Rahman asked the chiefs, elders, and others whose opinions were paramount. So, after dawn prayer, he addressed the people in the Masjid as people were waiting for the decision on who will be the *Ameer*. Ammar Ibn Yasir said it should go to Ali and Miqdad Ibnul Aswad supported him. But Abdullah Ibn Abi Sarah said it should go to Uthman and Abdullah Ibn Abi Rabee'a supported him, and the arguments began. So Sa'd Ibn Abi Waqas told Abdur Rahman to go ahead and finish the job, so the dispute would not be extended. Abdur Rahman asked Ali to come forward, and was asked, "I give you an oath by Allah that you shall follow the book of Allah, the Sunnah of his Prophet, and the practices of the two successors before you." Ali said he would do the best to his knowledge and power, and then Abdur Rahman asked Uthman and repeated to him the same oath. Uthman replied yes, and after that Abdur Rahman gave the pledge.

Then Uthman addressed the people and gave them religious advice. He told them about the temporary life of the world and the permanent life of the coming world. He also told them about justice, and kindness to others and especially he mentioned the *Zimmies*, the non-Muslim citizens in the state.

It is said that the reason Abdur Rahman gave the pledge to Uthman over Ali is because Ali did not give his response with surety, but to us that was not the only reason. Another reason is that the majority of the council selected by Umar voted in favor of Uthman and the majority of the chiefs and elders that Abdur Rahman asked were in favor of Uthman as well.

Later on, when rebels killed Uthman, people rushed to Ali and asked him to take over. However, Ali said, "this is yours? this is a case of the people of Badr," then he said, "where are Talha, Sa'd and Zubair?" So, they came and gave their pledge to Ali and then others followed soon after. This was the only way at that time because they were facing a situation with great turmoil due to the killing of Uthman.

While Ali was the *Khalifa*, he deposed a few of those who were appointed by Uthman, such as Muawiya Ibn Abi Sufyan, who was the governor of Sham. Muawiya refused the *Khalafah* of Ali by taking a plea for the retribution of Uthman first while Ali was of the view that they should wait and let the situation calm down. The reason Ali wanted the situation to calm down was because the actual killers are not known. This caused disputes and battles between the two parties, and when Ibn Muljim killed Ali, the Muslims gave their pledge to Ali's son Hassan. Battles continued between Hassan and Muawiya until Hassan's forces were defeated, and he saw the fighting would get worse. So, to stop the bloodshed Hassan withdrew from *Khalafah* and gave his pledge to Muawiya.

Now keeping in view, the historical context of the Sahaba, the scholars said that for the appointment of a *Khalifa* there are four ways.

(I) The "Bay'ah" of "Ahlul Halli Wal Aqd" as it was done in the case of the *Khalafah* of Abu Bakr.

(II) Appointment by the *Khalifa* as Abu Bakr did it in the case of Umar.

(III) Appointment of a *Shura* (council) to choose one from amongst them as it was in the case of the *Khalafah* of Uthman. This was supported by the public or to a great extent it was also in the *Khalafah* of Ali as well because he was sitting in the masjid for the general public to give him the pledge of allegiance.

(IV) To take over by force, as we can see in the case of Muawiya. In the Hanafi School of jurisprudence, the jurists say that the Khalifa could be appointed either through *Bai'at* or be nominated by the previous *Khalifa* or to become *Khalifa* by force (Radd Ul Muhtar). Ibn Humam said one could become a *Khalifa* either by the *Bai'at* of people of opinion (*Ahlul Halli Wal Aqd*) or by force (*Al Musayarah*).

Ibn Nujaym mentioned *Bai'at* only, but he implied force as well. As he said if someone gets into power by force, and he is doing wrong but has the control of the state. So, his deposition does not take place itself, and as he has power so if he does not listen to those who have the right to depose the ruler, he remains in power. Moreover, if he has lost the power then his *Bai'at* means nothing because for the *Khalifa*, two things are necessary:

(I) Ahlul Halli Wal Aqd must give him the pledge.

(II) He had the power and authority over the people to make them submissive to his order and rule.

In Maliki *Fiqh*, they also mentioned these three ways

    (I)   The *Bay'ah*

    (II)   The appointment by the previous *Khalifa*

    (III) Taking it by force (Ad Dusuqi with Ash Sharhul Kabeer) in Shafi *Fiqh* books. These three ways are also mentioned in Nihayatul Muhtaj and Tuhfatul Muhtaj. The Hanbali School also has the same view (Al Mughni, Kash'Shaful Qanna).

Allama Aamidi and Imam Ash'ari both mentioned only two ways

    (I)   The *Bay'ah*

    (II)   The appointment by the predecessor (Abkarul Afkar)

In *Al Mawaqif*, Allama Eiji also mentioned these two ways. However, Allama Qurtubi in his *Tafseer* mentioned all those ways that we have listed.

Hafiz Ibn Hazm said that the best way is appointment by the predecessor. According to Ibn Hazm, putting Abu Bakr on the prayer rug in his lifetime by the Prophet was the appointment for *Khalafah* and Abu Bakr did it in the case of Umar. This is a good way to avoid feuds and turmoil.

While some other scholars said that the case of Abu Bakr was not the case of appointment for Khalafah but he became *Khalifa* based on *Bai'at*, while Umar also became Khalifa with the *Bai'at* of the public, but on appointment by the predecessor, Ibn Hazm claimed an *Ijma* (consensus of jurists).

Allama Jawaini said that to ensure the legitimacy of *Khalafah*, it is not necessary for that all people in the state to approve it because Umar was proclaiming orders, and the news was not received by the people in the far-flung areas (*Al Irshad*). So, for him, the *Bai'at* of Ahlul Halli Wal Aqd is enough.

Shah Wali Ullah also mentions the four ways we mentioned, but he said they are:

(I)   *Bai'at* of Ahlul Halli Wal Aqd

(II) Appointment by the predecessor

(III) Appointment of a *Shura* to elect one from amongst them

(IV) Taking it by force

Now we say that in today's world the best practical way is the *Bai'at* of Ahlul Halli Wal Aqd and agreement of the people after that. Yes, in cases the appointment by the predecessor could be recommended, but:

(I)   THE APPOINTEE MUST HAVE THE REQUIRED QUALITIES FOR *KHALAFAH*.

(II) MUST BE CONSENTED TO BY THE PEOPLE

(III) THE APPOINTEE SHOULD NOT BE CLOSE FAMILY MEMBER OF THE PREDECESSOR.

As later the procedure could be abused, that is why Umar refused to put his son even in the candidature even though he was eligible. So, in abnormal circumstances this appointment can take place as well.

Khalafah by force gets its legitimacy as a necessity and situation because when he dethroned the *Khalifa* then it means that the *Khalifa* lost control of power, which is a requirement for *Khalafah*. this new one must have the qualities for a *Khalifa* and that Ahlul Halli Wal Aqd gave him the pledge and the people assented it as well. This is because people cannot dethrone this new leader by force, as he is the prevailing force, and also, he can implement the laws very well due to having power over the country.

Allama Sharbeeni said that if someone grabbed power by force then it is ok if he did it after the death of the *Khalifa* or got it from a *Khalifa* who was also a *Khalifa* by force; but if the first one was a *Khalifa* by appointment by his predecessor or by *Bai'at* then this type of *Khalafah* is not legitimate (*Mughinil Muhtaj*).

Jalaluddin Al Muhalli and Allama Ramali agreed with this view.

Ibn Qudamah, a Hanbali scholar, said that Abdul Malik Ibn Marwan killed Abdullah Ibn Zubair and then got *Bai'at* from the people of Makah and the areas of Ibn Zubair, and then a movement against him wasn't allowed because of the fear of bloodshed (*Al Mughni*).

So, in the life of the deposed one by force, the rule of the new one became all right because of the circumstances.

Hafiz Ibn Hazm said that at the time of the death the *Khalifa*, if someone got it by force, then that is ok if there is no one else to contest (*Al Fasl*). However, per the example he gave at the death of Uthman, Ali taking over by force does not make sense to us. This was not the case at all: Ali was a contestant with Uthman, and he also was the runner-up while Uthman was the winner, and now since Uthman died it was left for Ali to be the leader. Ali still wanted the public to come and approve his *Khalafah*, so he sat in the masjid and people came and assented to it.

Abu Yala related that the time of the tragedy of "Harrah" when Medina was attacked, Imam Ahmad led the prayer and said, "we are with the one who overtakes" (*Al Ahkam As Sultania*).

The reason is that the first *Khalifa* lost the power of the state, and now he can no longer protect and defend the people and their rights.

Allama Dusuqi said that when someone took over by force, then that is all right even if he lacks some of the required qualities because he must be able to save lives, defend rights, and maintain order (*Hashiyatul Dusuqi*).

Also, Allama Sharbeeni said that in case of taking by force, the *Khalafah* of an ignorant and a *Fasiq* is also all right.

Now another issue arises, is that is it all right to take power by force? Not at all but the proper procedure may then. In this regard, the best way is the Bai'at of Ahlul Halli Wal Aqd.

Some *Ulama* say that a *Khalifa* can appoint his father or his son as well. Other *Ulama* have said he can appoint his father but not his son, as the former will happen very rarely. However, in the case of the son the disadvantages are greater than the advantages, because the father is biased. However, *Jumhur* (the majority of scholars) said that it is not allowed for an immediate family like father, son, or brother to become rulers. They say this is like testimony in favor of one's kinfolk, and that is not accepted in Sharia.

Allama Aamidi said that the proper way is the *Bai'at* of Ahlul Halli Wal Aqd according to Sunnis, Zaidis, and Mu'tazilah (Abkarul Afkar).

However, as in a case of an appointment or grabbing it by force, the people give the pledge anyway. So actually, it becomes legitimate by that *Bai'at*, it becomes so because of the situation and under the doctrine of necessity.

The appointment of the *Shura* (Council) of six people to appoint one from amongst them by Umar was also a type of appointment according to Allama Mawardi. We say that was a combination of appointment and *Bai'at* of Ahlul Halli Wal Aqd. Imam Ghazali said that Abu Bakr, by appointing Umar, had given him a pledge, but that was a pledge of one person while *Bai'at* means to gather the opinions together. So, when other major Sahaba also did the same, it was approved. Umar himself said of anyone who gave Bai'at to someone without the Muslims that it means nothing. Abbas said to Ali that he should not have accepted the membership of that *Shura* (he meant that he should have appointed Ali). However, Ali said that it was a matter of due importance (*Al Muqaddimah, Mughinil Muhtaj*).

So *Istikhlaf*, or appointing someone for *Khalafah* without taking a *Bai'at*, is not legitimate. That is why when Banu Ummayyah started this trend of *Istikhlaf*, but with all their good and bad still they needed the *Bai'at*. They used to take it even though in most cases the people did not have their word to say but gave the pledge. Umar bin Abdul Aziz openly said from the pulpit that he had been appointed without his consent or the people's consultation. So, he left them free to choose their *Khalifa*. However, as a known pious, just, and trustworthy man, the people forced him to be the *Khalifa*.

In case of appointment, as long as the appointing Imam is alive, he can take it back, just like a will, where the testator can take it back as long as s/he is alive. But this is not a recommended way to appoint one's son, for example. However, if he does so, and the people later gave their pledge to him, then it becomes legitimate. Because that appointment by the *Khalifa* is only a promise by him. However, he must have the qualities at the time of that promise and at the time of *Bai'at*. Also, the one to whom it is promised may not have refused it expressly until the death of the promising one (the previous *Khalifa*).

If the promised one is not present at the time of the death of the *Khalifa*, then someone should be put in charge. Otherwise, whosoever is given the pledge by the people first is the *Khalifa*, and if he put a sequence, then it should be followed.

Imam Bukhari and other narrated the story of the battle of "Mu'tah" wherein the Prophet appointed Zaid Ibn Harith as *Ameer* (leading general) of that expedition. Moreover, said if he was martyred then Jafar would lead and, if he were also martyred, then it would fall to Abdullah Ibn Rawahah. When he was martyred, then Thabit Ibn Arqam grabbed the flag and said with a loud voice to the Muslims, to agree, however, to lead them. They said he should lead them, but he refused, so they agreed upon Khalid Ibn Waleed.

This story gives us the concept of three leaders, one after the other, even though this was an appointment for a specific duty. However, still as the practice of the Prophet and being a source of law gave us the basic concept. Also, that story gives us the way to choose the leader as well.

Regarding a *Khalifa's* appointment, witnesses are not necessary to legitimize it. However, as it may be the case that people will deny and say that no nomination has taken place, there should be witnesses to testify that the previous *Khalifa* has nominated this person.

For the battle of Nehawand, Umar also appointed Huzaifah Ibn Yaman and after him Numan Ibn Muqrin and in the battle of Jaser. Abu Ubaidah, the leading commander, said, "if I am killed then Jubair will lead, and in case of his martyrdom, Murr will lead the mission."

So, the nomination of someone for *Khalafah* by the previous *Khalifa* is a just candidate for *Khalafah*, as Umar became a legitimate *Khalifa* with *Bai'at* and Uthman was elected and given *Bai'at* by the Shura first. Hafiz Ibn Taymiyyah said so in his book *Minhajus Sunnah*. Moreover, when the appointed/nominated one has the required qualities, then this is preferred way according to Hafiz Ibn Hazm.

In brief, we can say that, like prophet-hood, the *Khalafah* cannot be inherited. Inheritance goes to the heir whether he is a good person or an evil one and whether the dead individual said so or kept quiet on the matter. Allah said:

"And (remember) when Abraham was tested by his Lord with a few kalimat (tests), he performed perfectly. He [Allah] said, Verily I am going to make you an Imam for people [humanity]. He [(Abraham] said and [make Imams] from my offspring. He [Allah] said, my promise will not include the wrongdoers." - (2:124)

AHLUL HALLI WAL AQD

It means the people of *Hall* and *Aqd*. Literally *Hall* means to untie, solution, analyze, or to resolve, while *Aqd* means to tie, conclude, ratify, or determine.

Keeping in view these meanings described above of these two words, these people, and their qualities in one way or the other, they can make knots and tie, and they can unite and resolve complicated issues and determine and ratify.

This term of Ahlul Halli Wal Aqd is very frequently used in Sharia and is defined as the people who select or elect an Imam and give him the *Bai'at* (pledge). Jalaluddin Muhalli said in his footnote in his book *Minhaj* that these people may have the qualities of a witness in Sharia to be just and honest, knowing the required qualities for *Khalifa* and to know that the one who will be elected has these qualities.

Allama Bahuti from the Hanbalis also mentioned this (*Kash'Shaful Qanna*). Al Mawardi gives them the title "Arbabul Ikhtiyar," or people who have the right to choose.

However, how are these Ahlul Halli Wal Aqd going to be determined? It all depends upon circumstances, situation, and culture. In Islamic Sharia, there are terms *Ijma* or *Olul Amr*. So, for *Ijma* they said that in *Fiqhi* issues it is the consensus of opinions of the jurists.

While for different fields there are different experts or leaders, and for the *Khalafah* it has two sides,

(I) RELIGIOUS SIDE

(II) WORLDLY SIDE

So, in *Ahlul Halli Wal Aqd*, both of these sides may be taken into consideration. So, the scholars said that *Ahlul Halli Wal Aqd* are the religious scholars, the chief of tribes, the social leaders, the people in authority, and the commanders. So, when such people agree with someone, and that is not against Quran and Sunnah, then it is binding to follow.

Regarding the numbers of *Ahlul Halli Wal Aqd*, there is no specific text, but it depends on the situation. When *Ahlul Halli Wal Aqd* ask an eligible person for the responsibility, but the person denies it, then they cannot force him because this is a contract that requires mutual consent. So, they must look for a person who is best qualified for the responsibility. Also, in this regard they must investigate the facts so they can decide which person should be given priority in such circumstances.

REQUIRED QUALITIES OF A

KHALIFA

How should a *Khalifa* be chosen? We have established the decision goes to *Ahlul Halli Wal Aqd*, and they will choose and give him a pledge then after that the public will ratify it. However, the important thing is who is eligible for *Khalafah*. Also, various departments inquire about his record; otherwise, they may reject him for the post even though the person is a qualified one, the post of *Khalifa* is the utmost high post and responsibility. So, on the one hand, the Khalifa is the agent of Allah to implement his rules, while on the contrary he is the custodian and guardian of the general public. How sensitive is this post? So, the *Khalifa* must have the following qualities:

1. MUST BE A MUSLIM,

Because he is the guardian of the *Deen* of Allah and he has to implement it, so if he does not believe in Islam, then how can he show sincerity to that *Deen*? This is just like secular laws that stipulate that a head of state must be a citizen of that country by birth and for other responsible posts to be a citizen by naturalization at least.

2. MUST BE ADL,

Which means he is an adult, and a sane and just person. He needs to be mature because he will command, judge, and guard the state, people, and their rights as well. Allah said:

> *"Do justice, that is closer/nearest to piety." - (5:8)*

> *"Verily Allah commands for justice and kindness." - (16:90)*

This justice by the people in authority is a must even in the case of an enemy.

Allah said:

> *"And let not the hatred of a people take you towards transgression because of that they have stopped you from Masjid Al Haram [to perform your worship]." - (5:2)*

That is the duty of a Muslim for Allah.

Allah said:

> *"O you who believe! Stand out firmly [be rulers] for Allah and be a just witness. Moreover, let not hatred of a people take you towards injustice. Do justice, that is nearest to piety and fear Allah, indeed Allah is all-aware of what you do." (5:8)*

> *"O you who believe! Stand out firmly [be rulers] for justice, witness to Allah even though it be against yourselves or your parents or your kin, be he rich or poor, Allah is prior to them both, so follow not the lusts*

so you may do justice and if you distort or turn your face, then Allah is all-aware of what you do" (4:135)

It became clear that in testimony and rule two things are necessary:

(I) TO BE JUST TO ALL

(II) TO BE FOR ALLAH

So, injustice or discrimination is not permissible. To be *Adl* or just is to be endowed with qualities like truth, trustworthiness, avoiding forbidden and disliked things and practices, and sins of every type, self-control in anger, avoiding any doubtful thing, having dignity in one's movements.

(III) **TO BE A JURIST,**

Since a *Khalifa* must implement the rules of Sharia. Sometimes situations come up that need an immediate response so if the Khalifa does not have the qualities of a *Mujtahid* (Jurist) then how will he deduce and respond? So, he must know the political, economic, cultural, and social changes as well because there are issues that do not exist in Quran and Sunnah but needs deduction. Or sometimes these rules are deduced but in a different situation, so when the situation changes a new deduction is needed. That is why *Khalafah* requires knowledge of Sharia and *Fiqh*.

> Note: By Sharia we mean the rules clearly mentioned in the text of the Quran and Sunnah or when *Ijma* has taken place; in this regard these rules are unchangeable. *Fiqh* here means the deduced laws and these are changeable but only by the authentic jurists. So, the *Khalifa* has to be a jurist because sometimes there is no time to consult a jurist.

(IV) TO HAVE STRONG WILLPOWER.

Whenever he finds anything good for the state and the people is found, then he neither feels fear nor does he fear any reaction but he goes ahead and makes it so.

Allah said:

> *O you who believe! Whoever from among you turn back from his* Deen, *then soon Allah will bring people, he will love them and they will love him, humble towards the believers, stern towards the disbelievers, striving hard in the cause of Allah and never afraid of the blame of a blamer." - (5:54)*

The rule will never take place with fear and even with reservations. In other words, it means he must be a brave and courageous person.

(V) SKILLED IN MILITARY STRATEGY AND TACTICS

Because he is the commander-in-chief. Otherwise, he will not be able to make a decision of war and peace.

(VI) BE A GOOD POLITICAL PLANNER

In a sense that he must know how to tackle different issues and resolve them, and the people must trust in him in this regard.

(VII) HE MUST BE MALE

When the daughter of the Persian emperor took over the kingdom, the Prophet of Allah said,

> "Never will a people enjoy success who turned over their affairs [state and government] to a woman (Bukhari).

Allah has given different qualities to different individuals and therefore all over the world, different responsibilities are granted to different individuals. Also, no one makes an objection to it as that is either given to them because of his or her natural ability or because of his or her earned qualifications. In the same way Allah, the Creator has given different qualities to different genders, you can observe that from their structure. Now observe how men usually have a commanding voice, while women have a soft one. Their structure also has similar differences. Allah said:

> "And do not covet that by which Allah has made some of you excel others, men shall have the benefit of what they have availed and women shall have the benefit of what they availed and ask Allah for his grace. Surely Allah is the all knower of everything." - (4:32)

This verse expressed that both men and women have their own spheres of achievement. Based on that, Allah has given them their specific responsibilities, and that is why to ask Allah for his grace means to empower you to fulfill your obligations. Why is this important? The answer is that the male and female genders are Allah's creation, and his decision and he is all-knower of everything.

There are rules and laws, like prayer or fasting, that apply to everyone, whether male or female, rich or poor, rulers or the average person. However, there are some rules and laws that differ from person to person based on their situation, like *Zakat* and charity, which are obligations for the rich but for the poor. Sometimes these laws depend on specific circumstances, even temporary ones: for example, when traveling, a person prays two *Rakat* instead of the usual four that are requited when at home.

A Muslim ruler is bound to implement the penalties of Sharia, but that is not the duty of the general public. These differences come about because they do not have the capability to do it or because it will cause a person hardship; the differences are not meant to deprive someone but to relieve them of some responsibility. Men, if they are of sound mind is sane, are obligated to pray. If a man cannot pray standing due to illness or infirmity, he must pray sitting. However, women are not required to pray when they are menstruating. Moreover, they are not required to fast at that time, but they must make up the fast later. It is the case of *Khalafah* and *Khalifa's* duties in Islam; it is not a right but a duty, and that is why the Prophet said that to be the ruler is a big test.

So, if *Khalafah* is considered a right, then not to have a woman as a *Khalifa* has to be a deprivation. However, when it is recognized a duty in Sharia, then the one who has been dropped from this tremendous responsibility should be happy. Moreover, that is why a God-fearing person, whenever he accepts so great a responsibility, becomes to worldly people a person of a high status. However, these God-fearing people does not receive congratulations for that; rather they should be consoled, even pitied. They even ask their well-wishers to make *Dua* (supplication) for them, so they are not held accountable for that on the Day of Judgment.

An important point to note is that throughout the world there is a vote by the public, and there is Parliament and the laws and rules are coming to the parliament and debated on. Moreover, then a due process takes place and after that the head of state signs the law, it becomes an act, which means that the head of state does not have absolute power. So if such a system exists, then can a woman be Head of the State or not? Also in a parliamentary form of government the head of the state is a symbolic leader while the chief executive is the prime minister.

Alternatively, in a constitutional monarchy, the king and/or queen are the symbolic heads of state. In this form of government, the prime minister is also the chief executive. In *Khalafah* the *Khalifa* is the head of the state and chief executive, and he is not subject to the Parliament, but he is only subject to Allah and his *Deen*. So, if a *Khalifa* is not of that perfect Islamic form, but of this democratic form of government, he does not have that status of head of the state and chief executive. Then what will be the *fatwa* (Islamic ruling) about the rule of woman? This is a question that must be answered because a woman may be in power and hold any position other than the *Khalifa*; the *Fuqaha* have not put any restrictions on that.

While in a democratic form of government s/he will be just like a spokesperson of the state and government, but still, it depends on what type of power s/he has. In the executive branch of the government the president has the veto power regarding any act or law, so there is some absolute power available to him/her as a president. However, Islam is a system, and that system must be taken into consideration. That the *Khalifa* is the agent of Allah, dually elected by *Ahlul Halli Wal Aqd* and approved, verified, and ratified by the public. The *Khalifa* must be their guardian, custodian, and servant and being the head of the state and chief executive and subject to Allah and his *Deen*. Then for such a person it is must to be a man, as such a huge burden may not be put on the shoulders of a woman. That will overburden her, and go against the softness of her nature, and against her dignity and natural decency.

(VIII) HE MUST BE SOUND IN MIND AND BODY

Allama Mawardi said, that defect in this regard is of three types:

A. Mental defect.

B. Physical defect.

C. A defect in power and freedom of action.

As for defect in senses is concerned, that is also of three types:

A. That defect which obstructs and prevent someone to be an Imam.

B. That defect which does not preclude one from being an Imam.

C. That defect regarding which there is a difference of opinion amongst the scholars.

Examples of the first one is insanity and blindness; of the second, the loss of smell or loss of taste. These latter two deficiencies do not have anything to do with being an Imam or a *Khalifa*, as they do not affect intellect or opinion. Examples of the third one includes deafness or mutism. These two prevent one from becoming a *Khalifa*, but if an Imam lost it after he became *Khalifa*, one group says, he must be deposed from his duty like in the case of blindness, as these both affect planning and action. Another group says that he can do his job with accommodations such as sign language. There is a third group that is of the view that if he can write then he is still fit for the job because writing is a clear method of expression, while sign language may still present some ambiguity. However, the first opinion is the preferred one.

As for the defect in organs is concerned, that is of four types:

A. That defect that neither makes him look bad nor affects his intellect and opinion, for example, if a man is circumcised, or he is castrated, or his ears are pierced. In this case, he could be chosen as *Khalifa*, and he can carry on his duty as *Khalifa* if he undergoes any of these procedures during *Khalafah*.

B. A defect in hands and/or legs. If both hands are amputated, then he cannot do anything, and if both his legs are amputated then he cannot stand. In such a circumstance, he cannot be chosen, nor can he carry on his business as Imam if these body parts were amputated when he was a *Khalifa*.

C. That defect with which he could not be chosen. However, if he was a *Khalifa*, and it happened to him then this becomes a disputed issue amongst the jurists. One group says he can carry on with his duty. While another group says, he cannot, and that is if one of his hands is amputated, or one of his legs is amputated.

D. That defect that does not affect the *Khalifa* to carry on as being the Imam. However, regarding candidature as Imam there are two opinions. One group says he can be chosen as Imam. While another opinion is that he cannot be selected as Imam. Moreover, the example is if his nose is cut off, or if he has one eye.

Moreover, as for defect in power and action is concerned, that is of two types:

(I) *Hijr* as in if some of his ministers took control from him in which he has the de facto power to do or undo a thing. So now if that is by Sharia, then those actions are acceptable, but if that is against Sharia, then those actions may not stand and in such a case the minister concerned must be deposed.

(II) *Qahr* as in, he is confined and imprisoned illegally by his enemy in such a way that he cannot set himself free. In this case, he cannot be a candidate for *Khalafah* but if he was *Khalifa* and then he was imprisoned, the entire *ummah* is bound to help release him, and if they became disappointed and give up their hope for his release, then he is deposed.

These are the details according to the Sunni school. There is another quality, and that is:

(IX) LINEAGE.

The *Khalifa* must be from Quraish, as Abu Bakr narrated the Hadith that the Prophet said, *"the Imams after me will be/may be from Quraish (Ahmad/Abu Yala/ Tabarani/ from Bukair Ibn Wahab)."* We say that this Hadith is interpreted as a news the prophet gave but still, we say no, but when Abu Bakr said it, they took it as a rule and order. So, then we say that the Prophet said that this *Amr* (*Khalafah*) would be in Quraish as long as they keep straight or as long as they implement the *Deen*. Also, the Prophet said, "be straight with Quraish as long as they are straight with you (Tabarani)." Also, Bukhari and Muslim narrated that people are the followers of Quraish, the Muslim for the Muslim and the non-believers for the non-believers. So, these Ahadith make it clear that as long as they are sincere to *Deen,* they should be the rulers but if it is otherwise then this leadership will go to others. Alternatively, the Prophet means that they have the power, so people follow them, and that is why he said the Muslim for the Muslim and the non-believer for the non-believer. Moreover, that is why Ibn Khaldun said that Quraish was mentioned because of their power, strength, and support at that time and majority of the people used to follow and obey them.

So now this following and obedience must be taken into consideration. Moreover, now there is not only one Islamic state but more than fifty. Maybe Quraish is not available everywhere, nor every person from Quraish is eligible for the post. Hafiz Ibn Taymiyyah said Quraish at that time were powerful people, and that is why the Prophet mentioned them (*Iqtidaa Us Siratil Mustaqeem*). Moreover, as we mentioned that Shiites say that the Imam is referred to by name by the Prophet and it is a must for the Imam to be holy and having miracles as well. Also, they say that if the best one amongst the *ummah* has not been appointed as Imam that the *Khalafah* is void and has no legitimacy.

AHLUSH SHURA

In the Holy Quran, Allah praised those who believed firmly and put their trust in Allah and mentioned their qualities as well. One of these qualities is

> *"And their Amr is by mutual consultation (Shura)."* - *(42:38)*

The word *Amr* has many meanings like affair, government, et cetera. In the battle of Uhud when the Prophet achieved victory and those who were appointed on a strategic mountain were told not to leave that spot no matter what happened. However, forty out of fifty said, "the battle is finished and our colleagues who fought the war and defeated the enemy and are now exhausted. However, they still are collecting the booty so we should join them to help." Even though their *Ameer* (leader) Abdullah Ibn Jubair told them, "We should wait until we receive a new order from the Prophet," they said, "there is no need "So they came down from that mountain and from their back the people of Makah attacked them and not only was victory changed to defeat for the Muslims but seventy Sahaba were martyred and their bodies were dismembered. Moreover, even the Prophet of Allah was injured severely. Allah blamed them for what they did, but the Prophet never said a single word of blame even implicitly. Allah said:

"So, with what [a great] mercy from Allah you have become lenient towards them and had you been rough hard-hearted they would have dispersed from about you, so pass over [their faults] and implore in the affairs and when you have done Azm then put trust in Allah. Certainly Allah loves those who put their trust [in him]." - (3:159)

What is *Azm*?

Let's first see the position of *Shura* then we will come to know the meaning of this term. First, we say that every individual who is an adult, sane person, having no legal, or judicial restriction on his actions, has the freedom to act and to deal with his or her affairs the way he likes, provided s/he does not violate the laws and rules or harms anyone. Yes, if s/he wants to ask the advice of someone expert in the field concerned that is appreciated. However, if s/he does not then nobody can force him or her to consult anyone because that is a personal issue and affair. However, if that is a matter of collective nature, then we will see if there is a clear rule from the Quran and Sunnah. Then there is no room for advice and consultation as there is no reasoning against the Quran and Sunnah, but advice and consultation are nothing but reason and intellectual approach and opinion. Moreover, whenever there are no clear instructions in the Quran and Sunnah and the issue concerned is of social and collective nature then *Shura* is the order of Allah and his messenger.

Khateeb Baghdadi narrated from Abu Huraira that the Prophet said, "Ask a clever one for advice and do not disobey him, otherwise you will feel ashamed." Imam Mawardi quoted a Hadith, "Seek help for your affairs with consultation" (*Adabu Deeni Wad Dunya*); The Prophet said, "Whose advice is sought, he is the trustee" (Abu Dawud and Tirmidhi). It means that whoever advice is sought he must give the right advice with full sincerity otherwise, it could be considered as a breach of trust.

The Prophet himself used to consult his companions. He did the same in the battles of Badr, Uhud, and Ahzab, et cetera. After the Prophet, his successors used to do the same as Abu Bakr did in the case of the compilation of Holy Quran, and Umar did with regards to the land of Iraq.

The question arises: who should be consulted?

Those people who have opinions based on their knowledge, experience, et cetera. Allama Qurtubi said that in religious affairs the scholars of religion should be consulted. They must be intellectual and knowledgeable in worldly affairs, and ideally must also hold some affection for the individual who is looking for his advice, because sincere advice needs love and affection.

> *Ibn Atiyah said that* Shura *is from the basic rules of law and Sharia and one who does not consult the religious learned people then it is must to depose him (Al Bahrul Muheet).*

Ibn Adi and Bayhaqi narrated that the Prophet said, "Allah and his Messenger do not need it, but Allah made it a mercy for my ummah." So the Prophet also used to consult in affairs having no divine rule therein.

Allama Thanaullah Panipatti said,

> "Shura means to bring out the knowledge about the best practice after their consideration and thinking (Al Wajeez)."

Allama Shaukani said *that* Shura *is the standard practice of the* ummah *(Fathul Qadeer).*

In Makah, even the Prophet used to consult with his Sahaba in Darul Arqam. The *Khalafah* of Abu Bakr was based upon a Shura held on the porch of Banu Sa'idah. Umar's *Khalafah* became final in the house of Abu Bakr after that Abu Bakr nominated him. Uthman's Khalafah was decided after consultation in "Darul Miswar" and Ali's case was decided based on *Shura* in the masjid of the Prophet.

Allama Panipatti said that *Umar in certain cases used to consult women as well (Tafseer Mazhari).*

Moreover, Umar said, *"There is no* Khalafah *but with* Shura*" (Kanzul Ummal).*

Then Allama Mawardi mentioned five qualities of Ahlulsh Shura (Adabud Deen Wad Dunya):

i. He must be an intellectual and reasonable person by nature and have practical experience. Reason without experience and experience without intellect are not beneficial.

ii. He must be firm in faith and righteous in deeds. Umar said, "Seek in *Deen* the advice of those who have the fear of Allah (*Seerat Umar* by Ibnul Jawzi). Moreover, for sure he must be a scholar of *Deen*, otherwise, how will he give an opinion or advice? The fear of such people comes from the fact that they know Allah's power and accountability. Allah said:

"Indeed those who fear Allah from amongst his servants are only those who have knowledge." - (35:28)

iii. They must be free of worries and grief because it disturbs proper thinking. So at least financially, he should be in good condition.

iv. He must be a man of opinion, who loves people, and whom people love.

v. Regarding the issues he is giving his opinion on; he may not have a personal agenda, as that will be a conflict of interest and humans are weak by nature so he will be looking towards his personal benefit.

IS THE *SHURA'S* ADVICE ON THE *KHALIFA* BINDING?

It is the *Khalifa* who chooses his own Shura. Now this is another issue: how will he select his *Shura*? Does it depend on when the *Shura* gave its opinion what about its acceptance and implementation? There is nothing in the Quran and Sunnah that explicitly says that the *Ameer* is bound to follow the *Shura* or avoid it. Hafiz Ibn Kathir related from Ali that the Prophet was asked about the word *Azm* in the verse

> "When you did Azm then put your trust in Allah." - (3:159)

So, he said that it is consultation with the people of opinion and to follow that, but we say that depends. If the *Ameer* thinks that the view of the majority is good for the *ummah*, then he will go for that. Moreover, if the opinion of the minority is right for them, then he will choose that opinion. Even if he has a third opinion of his own that is better to his knowledge, thinking, experience, and situation, then that way should be preferred. This is because in Islam, priority is not given to quantity but rather to quality. Allah said:

> "And if you obey most of those on earth, they will mislead you far away from the path of Allah. They follow

> *nothing but conjecture, and they do nothing but an estimation." - (6:116)*

Yes, we can say that the people within the *Shura* are not like this and should not be like this, but still, they are human. So, we say that *Shura* is a discussion and debate in order to make different sides of that issue for the *Ameer* to decide. It is very similar to the debate, discussion, and arguments of the two opposing attorneys in a trial, who make the issue clear to the judge and court to make a proper ruling. It does not mean that the judge puts his or her knowledge and experience to the side. Rather s/he takes all these into consideration and then decides and makes his or her ruling.

While for a *Khalifa* to decide based on his opinion. His thinking is more suitable like a veto by a president or head of the state, or perhaps like an executive order.

In verse 3:159 Allah said after consulting

> *"So when you did Azm, the word Azm is in the singular form and not in a plural one."*

Which means that this *Azm* (strong will) comes from an individual. Also, Allah said "then put your trust in Allah," which embodies that. Yes, sometimes there will be reservations because a majority or sometimes even all the *Shura* will agree on an issue but the *Khalifa* decided otherwise.

That is why Allah said,

> *"Do not look at that but go ahead and put your trust in Allah."*

Moreover, strong will means that even if the majority is against you, it still does not cause you to falter. Umar sometimes used to give priority to the opinion of Ibn Abbas, even though the majority of Sahaba said otherwise. Even the Prophet often used to give priority to the views of Abu Bakr and Umar against the majority of Sahaba. Even some of the Sahaba were of the opinion that verse number 3:159

> *"And consult them in the affair, meant to consult Abu Bakr and Umar only, and that was according to Ibn Abbas." (Hakim)*

Imam Ahmad narrated a Hadith that the Prophet said to them

> *"If you both had got together on an opinion, I would not have opposed that."*

Ibn Sad narrated from Umar that people asked him if something is not there in the Quran and Sunnah, what should they do then? Umar said, "get opinions and decide it based on the majority." However, we say it depends, because if we make the *Khalifa* subject to the *Shura* then that is a contradiction.

One point to mention is that nowadays when democracy is introduced by the developed and powerful countries the people are influenced by it. Then undoubtedly the Muslims will have some reservations about this Islamic system in the light of Quran and Sunnah about that but this is not a democracy.

Each and every man-made system in human history has its background. Mostly that come into existence as a reaction to another thing, like communism, which came as a reaction to capitalism, and that is why the thinkers said that communism is the virulent form of western capitalism.

Likewise, the whole world was in the grip of cruel kingships and aristocracy, and democracy came into existence as a reaction to that. So, there may not be the rule of an individual but rather to the public, just like communism said there is no property of an individual but rather of the community. So, the general public has been given such freedom that they have no time to think of the Creator, His Lordship, or even His rules. However, Islam has given the right of a government to the public but as agents of Allah, subject to his supremacy and sovereignty. So even the *Khalifa* is going to represent the public in one way and Allah in the other. Which makes the *Khalifa's* job very sensitive and very careful. As an agent, he is not the ruler but Allah is, and he is not a ruler but an agent and servant of the public. That is why God-fearing people would run away from the responsibility of being *Khalifa*. Those that became *Khalifa* used to feel sorry for themselves. Like Abu Bakr when he saw a bird singing, he started crying and said:

> *"What a lucky creature you are, flying freely from one branch to another eating wherever you wish to sing and enjoying, you will die, and that is the end. No accountability, no judgment, no punishment- but I would be put to accountability, and Allah knows better what will happen as a* Khalifa *as I would be questioned about everyone."*

Moreover, Umar said, *"even if a dog died hungry on the shore of the Euphrates River, Umar would be asked about that also."*

At the time of his death, he was asked by the major Sahaba to nominate his son. He became upset and said for the family of Umar it is more than enough that only one person would be questioned about the due rights of the people. Moreover, if I am rescued even without a reward for that, then I am the luckiest person.

So, as we said that each and every system is like a culture to be taken as a whole. For example, a combination of medicines will show their effect only when the sick person takes it as a package, otherwise they will not work. Moreover, even democracies in different parts of the world take various forms because of the prevailing cultures and the circumstances people are living in. However, they are all based on secularism and the rule of the public. In Islam, on the other hand, the government is based upon the sovereignty of Allah. The supremacy of Quran, Sunnah, and the rule of the general public as agents of Allah and the role of the *Khalifa* as an agent of Allah and the public at large.

AHLUL IJTIHAD

By the term Ahlul Ijtihad, we do not mean the jurists and *Fuqaha*, but rather we mean the technocrats. Especially nowadays when each and every subject and technology has become a specialty and issues arise, so an expert opinion is a must. There are two basic qualities needed for such a person:

(I) He must be an expert technocrat of that field and subject

(II) He must be a trustworthy person and give his expert opinion with full sincerity. Allah said:

"Then ask Ahlul Zikr *[experts] if you do not know."* - *(21:7)*

Now there are three types of people:

1. *Ahlul Halli Wal Aqd*: they will select, nominate, and elect the Khalifa.

2. *Ahlulsh Shura*: they would be consulted.

3. *Ahlul Ijtihad* or the expert and technocrats for expert opinion.

These three altogether constitute the parliament/assembly/ consultative council and legislative body. How to appoint them? It depends on circumstance and situations.

RIGHTS AND DUTIES OF THE KHALIFA

As we know, *Deen* itself is rights and responsibilities because Deen is for humans as they are social by nature, living with one another and that is why everyone has his rights and his duties as well. Mostly the rights of one person are the obligations of the others and vice versa when it comes to interactions, it is the case of the *Khalifa* and the general public. Both have duties, and both have rights as well. However, as *Khalifa* has a big responsibility, so we will mention his duties first and then the rights.

DUTIES OF *KHALIFA*

The obligations of the *Khalifa* are as follows:

A. PROTECTION OF DEEN

This is the first one and most important duty of the Khalifa as we mentioned in the definition of Khalafah that it is the protection of Deen and planning of this world.

B. TO ESTABLISH A JUSTICE SYSTEM

As we mentioned before that justice is the commandment of Allah.

Allah said:

> "Indeed Allah commands Adl [justice]." - (4:58)

> "Indeed we sent our messenger with the scripture and scale so that people may stand with justice." - (57:25)

It means that the purpose of the message of all the messengers was the balance, and justice takes a person close to piety.

Allah said:

> "Administer justice, which is nearer to piety." - (5:8)

> *"O you who believe! If you fear Allah, he will give you* Furqan *criteria (the distinction between right and wrong)." - (8:29)*

To establish justice is the purpose of the state, government, and authority. That is what Abu Bakr said in his first address as *Khalifa*:

> *"Truth is just/trust while a lie is a type of fraud. Moreover, the weak one is strong near me; I take his right if Allah wills and the strong one is weak near me till take the right [of others] from him if Allah wills."*

This is justice, that nobody may be deprived of their rights.

C. TO PROTECT THE STATE AND TO PROVIDE AND ESTABLISH PEACE

Khalafah is based upon a state. So that base must be protected and defended, and the general public must be provided with peace. That they can contribute to the social, economic, and political life of the state and society, which will further strengthen the state. It means that integrity of the state and peace for the people both depends upon one another. In other words, we can say that his duty is to make the state a welfare one and a welfare state is based on two things:

I. Availability of needs and necessities

II. No fear of any type (peace).

These two also depend upon one another as wherever the basic needs and necessities are not easily available to people. So, there can be no peace and where every there is no peace, for sure there will be no availability for basic needs and necessities as people will not move or work freely. That is why the Holy Quran mentioned these two things jointly in three places. Allah said:

1. *"And we will put you to test with a little but fear and hunger." - (2:155)*

2. *"Moreover, Allah put forward the example of a township that dwelt secure and well content, its provision was coming to it in abundance from every place but it denied the favors of Allah, so Allah made it taste the extremes of hunger and fear because of that which they used to do." - (16:112)*

3. *So they [Quraish] may worship the Lord of the house [Kaba] who has fed them against hunger and has made them safe from fear." - (3:106)*

In a state, hunger will go away if agriculture, business, and manufacturing are running smoothly and successfully, and that will be possible if there are peace and peace will come when justice is not only administered but that is clearly seen, and everyone believe that injustice would never be done to me. If peace is not there, then the state will be a security state and not a secure state. A welfare state is a secure state.

D. TO CARRY OUT PUNISHMENT ON CRIMINALS

Human beings have desires, and they are living in a world of desires. They have wishes, lusts, and anger as well. Because of those faults, sometimes they attack the life, property, and honor of others. If it is not controlled, then it will spread disorder, mischief, turmoil, and bloodshed, and soon the state will lose its control. The government will not have its grip over the country anymore; in other words, the *Khalafah* will not remain anymore. So, Islam has fixed some punishment and regarding these punishments Allah stated that it is a prevention of these crimes. Allah said:

"And for you in Qisas *[retribution] there is life, O people of understanding so you may avoid [killing]." - (2:179)*

"And a man who committed theft and a woman who committed theft cut off their hands (the right hand from the wrist) as a recompense for what they have done, as a chastisement (warning) from Allah and Allah is Allmighty, All-wise." - (5:38)

The purpose of punishment and the wisdom therein is the protection of the society, as Islam is not eager to punish people but to implement such a thing, which is better for the public in general. All these crimes are not only harmful to people, but that is an insult of the sacred orders of Allah as well, who is the supreme and sovereign Lord of the universe.

E. TO PROTECT THE BOUNDARIES OF THE STATE

For example, when two individuals are living together, sometimes a dispute arises. Sometimes one of them wants to grab the property of the other or attack him because of their ego. The same thing happens to two states as well, and maybe one of them will try to annex a part of the other's country. So, the *Khalifa* is bound to defend and protect the borders. To strengthen the boundaries means to protect the citizens.

The Prophet said

"To guard the boundaries [of the state] for one day and night is better than the [whole] world and whatever therein"

Allah said:

> *"O you who believe, fear Allah, be stable and enjoin one another to be stable and do* Ribat *[guarding the borders] and fear Allah to enjoy success." - (3:200)*

F. STRIVING HARD AGAINST THOSE WHO CONSPIRE AGAINST ISLAM

As we said, people by nature hold enmity against one another for known or unknown reasons, and there also will be conspiracies coming from outside and sometimes from within, so the *Khalifa* must be alerted to counter these conspiracies. In the Holy Quran, it is called *Fitnah*, which means a conspiracy, sedition, treason, plot, or even an attack. Allah said:

> *"And fight them till there is no "Fitnah" [remaining]"* (2:193 and 8:39).

Jihad is a binding duty of Muslims for the said reason. Moreover, as *Fitnah* will happen until the last day,

the Prophet said,

> *"Jihad will be going on until the day of judgment."*

We can say that Jihad is against *Harabah* which means an actual fight broke out, or a plot for an attack is being planned, so the state is bound to counter and to defuse that.

G. TO ESTABLISH EXCHEQUER (BAITUL MAL)

The state has expenses and needs revenue. For the said purpose, it must have a system to get that from legitimate sources.

So, *Baitul Mal* has four branches:

A. Collecting 1/5th of mining and booty.

Allah said:

> *"And know that whatever of war-booty that you have gained, verily 1/5th of it is assigned to Allah and to the Messenger, the relatives of the Messenger, to orphans, the poor who beg, and to the wayfarer." - (8:41)*

Mines are naturally found in the earth and according to the Hanafiyyah that is of three types:

(I) A metal that can be melted, like gold, silver, copper, et cetera.

(II) Minerals that cannot be melted, like precious stones.

(III) Liquids like petroleum and other types of oil.

The melting mines if needed for government and the general public, then it may not be allotted to anyone but rather it goes to the exchequer. However, if that is found by the citizen in a land and does not belong to anybody, then 1/5 of the booty will go to the national revenue, while the solid one will go to the person concerned as that is considered similar to stone and dirt. Also, the liquid type is like water; that will go to the person that found it except mercury as that is a melted type so 1/5 of it would go to the national revenue. If the melting mine is discovered in a land that has an owner, then it belongs to him as a whole. However, if found by other than the owner, then 4/5 will go to the owner and 1/5 to the finder. While according to Abu Yusuf and Muhammad in all these mines 1/5 will go to the revenue.

There is another thing called *Kanz*, and that is something buried by humans or buried underneath rubble due to a disaster. That will be either Islamic or not according to Islam, and thus depends on the circumstance. The first one is like found property: it must be announced, and if the owner is found he is entitled to it. Otherwise, it will go to the poor who are eligible for *Zakat*. Moreover, if that is from the time of non-Muslims, then its 1/5 will go to Baitul Mal and the remaining

4/5 to the very finder. However, Abu Yusuf said if that is found in an un-owned land then the whole thing goes to the finder while according to Abu Hanifa and Muhammad 1/5 of that will go to Baitul Mal.

Things coming out of the sea and ocean will go to the finder in full. That is the view of Abu Hanifa and Muhammad while the view of Abu Yusuf is that 1/5 goes to *Baitul Mal*.

According to Imam Malik, minerals like gold and silver go to *Baitul Mal* if found in an un-owned land, while if found in an owned land that still goes to the *Baitul Mal*.

Imam Shafi and Imam Ahmad said oil mines would go to the state, but a mine that needs labor to separate it from the earth, like gold and silver, go to the finder.

- B. *Sadaqat* like the *Zakat* of cattle, 1/10 or 1/20, of the crops as the case maybe and the business tax being taken from Muslim business people.

- C. *Kharaj* and *Jizyah*: *Kharaj* is the revenue tax of agricultural land from a non-Muslim and *Jizyah* is an annual tax that is taken from a non-Muslim for his property's protection. The tax is also taken from non-Muslim citizens or foreign businesspeople. Likewise, are the gifts given by the non-Muslims that are not citizens and the *Fay* (goods that come to Muslims without any war but as a peace treaty, and that will go to *Baitul Mal* in full).

- D. Regarding lost items or the property of those who die without heirs, the first two types will go to the people that are eligible for zakat as,

Allah said:

> *"Verily* Sadaqat *are only for the poor [who do not beg] and poor [who beg] and those employed to collect [these funds] and for the people that are inclined to Islam in order to attract them, and to free the captured and for those in debts and in the path of Allah and the wayfarer." - (9:60)*

The third category of collection is for public structure and welfare like roads, bridges, schools, hospitals, et cetera, as well as for the salaries of public servants. Even the needs of their families and children would be provided for from this while the fourth category is to pay the debts and duties of those in need.

Yes, the state can levy other taxes according to its needs and necessities but they must be reasonable and affordable. Heavy taxes not only destroy business, agriculture, and industry, they also create hatred towards those in power and eventually the state and the *Khalifa* as well.

E. To fix the salaries and allowances - as we know, the *Khalifa* is the shadow and shield of the state and people, but he alone cannot rule over all matters of state. He needs others to whom he can delegate certain powers and duties as well. The services of the state and public and working for them so that he may be given his wages on a reasonable basis. It depends on, as Imam Abu Dawud related a Hadith that the Prophet, said;

> *"Whosoever is our Aamil ([worker/collector]) he may have a wife [this means marriage expenses, then family expenses] and if he has no servant he may have a servant, and if he has no residence, so he may arrange a house."*

This means all his needs and necessities can and should be met. Shah Wali Ullah said that appointing officials depends upon the situation, circumstance, and needs. For example, during population increases, resources are enriched and discovered and relations with other countries are extended. That is why more and more departments and workers are needed, but a smaller number of employees and officials will mean the expense will be a lot less as well. Otherwise, that will overburden the national exchequer, which will cause an economic disaster. According to Shah Wali Ullah, this disaster has two causes:

I. Taking from the national exchequer in one name or the other

II. Imposing heavy taxes on those who are working

This second one discourages them from working, and they eventually desert their job and profession, so the income of the state decreases day by day while the Exchequer is drained.

Later on, for some time the state may be taking loans and soon it will become a defaulter state.

However, still Shah Wali Ullah said that five types of people are the basis of the system:

(I) **EXECUTIVE**

Humans by nature will attack one another, taking the properties or even the lives of one another. So, an executive body must be there to keep an eye on and control the people. If they have done any wrong, they may be taken into custody to bring them to law and justice. This department will try to maintain peace and order. They must be alert, strict, and diplomatic.

(II) **JUDICIARY**

As we mentioned before, justice is the commandment of Allah and his Messenger and naturally that is needed. Moreover, when there is no one to hold a wrongdoer to accountability then there will be no end to injustices. For the purpose above, the judges and judiciary are a must. We will discuss this in a special chapter Inshallah.

(III) REVENUE AND FINANCE

As we mentioned before in the topic of *Baitul Mal.*, the state has lots of expenses, which are supposed to be paid for by the public and from the state's resources.

(IV) ARMY

The state needs protection and defense, and the *Khalifa* is the supreme commander of the state and its forces. So, he will appoint the chief of the army, and that chief must have the required qualities and qualifications.

(V) SHAH WALI ULLAH HAS MENTIONED A FIFTH PERSON TO BE APPOINTED TO TAKE CARE OF THE FAMILY AFFAIRS OF THE *KHALIFA*

The *Khalifa* be provided with an atmosphere free of any worries, so he may have time to think freely about the state and the public. In other words, someone should be appointed to take care of his immediate family. Furthermore, with the passage of time other departments could be needed.

H. HE MUST KEEP HIMSELF UPDATED WITH STATE AFFAIRS AND THE PUBLIC.

Whatever the officers or the general public do, will have its effects on the state. Whether good or bad, it eventually led to the *Khalifa* himself. So, he must not have blind faith in the officials. He must be aware of what they do and how they do things. This is what we mean by the wording that the *Khalifa* must be the best planner. He must protect the *Deen* and discipline the worldly affairs. Not only this, but one who did wrong must be punished, and one who did good should be rewarded. So, they may be very alert no to do any wrong and anxious to do more and more good.

I. **HE MAY LISTEN TO SINCERE ADVICE FIRST** he has to recognize who the sincere one is. Unfortunately, the rule and rulers have the mentality that they like those who praise them a lot and flatter them, and they do not like those who tell them their faults. Imam Bukhari narrated a Hadith that the Prophet said, " *Deen* is *Naseehah* (sincerity). They said to whom? The Prophet said, to Allah, to his Messenger, to the Muslims in general, and to their Imams [leaders]". For the said purpose, he should appoint truthful and sincere people.

Now all these duties, which Imam Mawardi has mentioned, are a must to have the objects of Khalafah achieved. However, these are not limited to these ten as nature is evolutionary, change inevitable, so whatever is a must for the benefit of the state and public becomes the duties of the *Khalifa*.

Ibn Khaldun mentioned that all the rules and laws of Sharia are the responsibility of the *Khalifa* to take care of, to implement, and to convince the people to follow it whenever and wherever it is needed (*Al Muqaddimah*).

Shah Wali Ullah has classified these duties into two categories

(I) *DEEN* (RELIGIOUS) AFFAIRS.

(II) POLITICAL AFFAIRS.

"Religious matters" means to keep an eye on the public to ensure that they follow the laws and rules of Sharia. "Political affairs" means to defend the state, to control crime and to adjudicate disputes. In Islam all these are:

(I) CHAPTER OF *MAZALIM* (VIOLATIONS AND CRIMES)

(II) PENALTIES AND PUNISHMENTS

(III) JUDICIARY

(IV) JIHAD

Then the basic principles are mentioned in the Quran and Sunnah while the interpretation and deduction are left to the jurists, because disputes and differences in principles are disastrous but in interpretation and deduction is ease and a mercy of Allah. So, politics is a part of *Deen* as in Islam, *Deen* is not the personal business of someone, but that is a complete system. Allah said:

> *"Verily this Quran guides towards that [path of life] which is perfectly straight [and balanced] and gives glad tidings to the believers who practice righteous deeds that for them there is a great reward." - (17:9)*

This means that Quranic guidance will give a balanced, peaceful life here in this world and a prosperous one in the hereafter. Moreover, that is what a Muslim is looking for, and they invoke Allah and say

> *"O our Lord, give us good in this world, and good in the other world." - (2:201)*

The Prophet of Allah said

> *"That Bani Israel got led by their Prophets whenever one Prophet passed away another succeeded him [until this came to me], and there is no Prophet after me but will be the successors." - (Bukhari)*

Shah Wali Ullah said that the purpose of the message of Islam was to stop the wrongs towards others. Moreover, these wrongs could be either on the lives of others or their properties or their body. Also, for its protection and punishment came the retribution and penalties. So, the responsibility of the *Khalifa* is the protection and defense of the state. Moreover, when the state is Islamic, the people are Muslims and the ruler is Muslim as well. Then within that state there will not be any law other than Islam. Umar said the purpose of all these officials that have been appointed was to teach this *Deen* and to implement it.

Some scholars have mentioned some other duties of the *Khalifa*, and these are the basic needs and necessities to be provided to the public. These are listed under:

1. FOOD, CLOTHING, AND SHELTER

These are the basic needs of each and every living creature and every living creature by nature is looking for it, and that is called struggle for existence. Birds, animals, and even insects are constantly looking for food and shelter. Islam is natural and a natural system, so it does not press natural needs. Rather it polishes the ways looking for and command to make it easy to the approach of people. As we said that anyone who works for the state has the right to have a house and manage it as well. Even in the Islamic state within the basic needs there is no distinction and difference for anyone. Allah said:

> "He is the one who created all that is in the earth for you all" (2:29).

Which means that everyone has this right to live.

2. TO PROVIDE MEDICAL TREATMENT

The Prophet of Allah said, "Allah has not sent down any disease, but he has sent down for that disease a healing" (Bukhari). The Prophet himself not only used to take medicine but sometimes he used it to treat others. Ahmad, Tirmizi, and Abu Dawud related that they asked the Prophet regarding treatment, so the Prophet said, do the treatment.

Sickness and diseases are part of the natural system and so treatment is a core need of every individual.

3. EDUCATION

Allah has given animals senses, and they find and know things by using these senses. However, Allah has given *Aql* (intellect and reason) to the human being as a means and a source for further knowledge. Through this sense, the human being is utilizing the world. The resources of the earth are subjugated to him. Also based on intellect, Allah has made him bound to follow and obey his orders and commandments and these orders and commandments came to him through the messengers and revelation, which is the third source of gaining knowledge.

Allah made it clear to the angels that the Prophet Adam was the *Khalifa* of Allah through the knowledge and findings of Adam, as the angels said

> *"Do you appoint there in this [earth] on who will spread disorder therein and will shed blood while we do glorify you along with your praise and sanctify you. Allah said verily I know what you do not know. He [Allah] taught Adam the names of all that [put it in his nature]. Then he presented these to the angels and said, "tell me about the names of these [along with its use] if you are but truthful." They said, "glory be to you. There is no knowledge with us but only that which*

you have taught us-verily you are the all-knower, all-wise." He said, "O Adam! Inform them about the names of these," and when he told them about the names of these [along with its use as that was his natural requirements and necessity is the mother of invention and that's why humans are eager for research and invention and furthermore knowledge)]. He said, have I not told you that indeed I know what you reveal and what you used to conceal." - (2:30-33)

Then Allah insisted upon seeking knowledge regarding worldly gains and *Deen* as well. The word *Taskheer*, which means "subjugation," is used very frequently in the Holy Quran and Allah has subjugated to you whatever is in the world, which is an implicit order to use it. Allah said:

"And He (Allah) has subjugated to you the ships that they may sail in the sea by his command, and he has subjugated the river to you. Moreover, he has made the sun and the moon both constantly pursuing their courses to be of service to you. Moreover, he has subjugated the night and the day, and he gave you what you asked for [needed] and if you want to count the blessings of Allah you cannot count it [as that is countless] verily man is an extremely wrongdoer, extremely ungrateful" - (13:32-34)

"O Assembly of Jinn and Human! If you can pierce [penetrate] wherein the diameters of the heavens and the earth, then piercing [penetration] can only be done with power." - (55:33)

Allah did not put restrictions, rather he ordered us to do so, but he made it clear that his could only be possible if you have power. Allah said:

> *"He is the one who made the earth subservient to you, so go there on its shoulders and to him is the resurrection." - (67:15)*

All these depend upon further knowledge, research, science, and technology. This further research will make things easier to understand even regarding *Deen* as, Allah said:

> *"Soon we will show them our signs in the universe and their selves until it becomes manifest to them that this [Quran] is the truth, was it not sufficient in regard to your Lord that he is a witness [all-knower] of everything." - (41:53)*

Even though the Quran is not a book of science, certain scientific things are mentioned in it. The world is approaching these facts now and finding it through their research, and they will say "oh, the Quran mentioned that already." So, if now they believe in these facts based on their own research and knowledge then why did they not believe in that based on revelation, which was revealed by Allah the All-Knower?

The first revelation revealed to the Prophet said:

> *"Read in the name of your Lord who created. Who created the human from a clot. Read and your Lord is the* Akram *[more generous and respect giver]. The one who taught with the pen. Who taught human that which he did not know." - (96:1-5)*

Here Allah did not mention what to read. Of course, the first and most critical is the Quran and the matters of *Deen* but it also means read whatever is of benefit for you and people in general. Also, he ordered people to read those passages twice and mentioned that he is a generous and respectful giver. His generosity is that he will give you whatever knowledge you want, and respect is based on the pen, which is the mean and source of knowledge and education. Allah said:

> *"Say [O Muhammad] are those who know and those who do not know equal? None can understand this but people of understanding." - (39:9)*

Again, in this verse Allah did not mention what to know. So of course, *Deen* and its sciences are the priority but other sciences are meant as well. The only thing, which Allah ordered in the Quran to ask for, is an increase in knowledge

> *"And be not in haste [O Muhammad] with the Quran before its revelation is completed to you, and say, my Lord! Increase me in knowledge." (20:114)*

The Prophet ordered Zaid Ibn Thabit to study Hebrew. Among the captives of Badr those who had knowledge of writing, the Prophet ordered them to teach that to the youth of Medina and in exchange they would be released. So, this is the state's and *Khalifa's* responsibility to make education available to the people. In Islam, education is not a privilege but a right, as education makes people better and brings respect and dignity not only to the individuals themselves but also to society as a whole.

4. EMPLOYMENT AND JOBS

This is another duty of the state and *Khalifa* to establish and provide such an atmosphere where everyone can earn his livelihood in a respectable way. The Khalifa has to encourage agriculture, livestock, business, and industry. The Prophet, when receiving the first *Wahi* (revelation), came home shivering, and his wife Khadija consoled him saying,

> *"I swear by Allah, Allah will never put you down. Verily you take care of your kin, carry the burden [with patience or by carrying the burden of others], and you provide work to the jobless, you show hospitality to the guests, and you help in the right cause" (Bukhari).*

So, the Prophet, even before the message of Islam, used to arrange jobs for others. Also, Islam does not encourage begging but rather giving. Imam Bukhari narrated a Hadith of the Prophet about a man who takes his rope and brings a bunch of wood on his back and sells it. Allah protects his face with that, is better for him than asking people that sometimes they are giving him something and other times they are not giving anything.

Also, the Prophet said,

> *"The upper hand is better than the lower hand. The upper hand is the spending one while the lower hand is the begging one." (Bukhari and Muslim)*

Anas said, "that one Ansari came to the Prophet asking for help, The Prophet asked him if he has anything at home, the man said a cloak and a [wooden] cup. The Prophet told him to bring it. The man brought it, and the Prophet auctioned that for two dirhams and gave it to him and said, "give one to your family and buy an ax with the second dirham and bring it to me. The Prophet put a plank of wood under the ax and told him to cut the wood and sell it, and that he did not want to see the man for fifteen days. The man went and after those fifteen days he came back with ten dirhams, so he bought food and clothes. The Prophet said, "this is better for you than having a dot [a bad sign of begging] on your face on the day of resurrection" (Abu Dawud).

Shah Wali Ullah has mentioned that the state is bound to look into the scope of different fields and to arrange for jobs, otherwise the system will be disturbed as if all the people or a majority of them go for business and abandon the agriculture and livestock that provide for the business and industry, which will lead to starvation. He said that agriculture, which is the base, might be like flour used to make bread and that industry and business are like the salt in bread. All these must be organized and disciplined by the state. Moreover, if everyone is not provided with opportunity to earn, then the state is bound to give him welfare and allowance, otherwise he will resort to unsavory activities to earn money, which will harm the society at large and spread mischief and disorder.

Umar saw a non-Muslim begging and asked him, "what is this self-humiliation? The man said, "I have to pay the *Zimmah* (the tax imposed on non-Muslim citizens) but I am old and I cannot work." Umar, therefore, ordered that the *Zimmah* be waived after the age of sixty years, and the elderly must be provided sufficient welfare for themselves and their families. Umar said, "we have not done justice to him [the old man] if we have eaten his youth, and then put him down in his old age".

So, one who does not have some source of income, even though he is looking for one or he cannot do a job anymore, must be provided with sufficient revenue by the state. Umar was the first one to introduce this system in human history. Some Scandinavian countries still refer to this law of welfare as the "Umar Law".

5. ESTABLISH TRANSPORTATION INFRASTRUCTURE.

To establish and provide means of traveling and transportation: the state is bound to develop roads, bridges, and methods of transportation to make traveling convenient. The easier the movement of people, the stronger the society becomes and the more stable the economy becomes. Also, free movement is one of the fundamental rights of the citizen, so it must not only be secured but also improved to make it much easier.

6. TO MAKE MARRIAGE EASIER

The distinction of Muslims and the Muslim state is a noble character and a high level of morality. Islam insists upon noble character because character controls people not to violate the limits set by Allah and not harm individuals or society as a whole. The causes for immorality are two (I) Lust (II) Libido, in other words, the stomach, and the private parts. The Prophet of Allah said, "Whoever marries a pious woman has arranged the protection for half of the *Deen* so that he may fear Allah for the remaining half" (Bayhaqi). Also, the Prophet said, "This world is sweet and green, and verily Allah is making you an agent of his so he may see how you act, so fear the world [wealth] and fear women" (Muslim).

This Hadith means two things are dangerous, lust and the libido. As hunger and thirst, libido is a natural demand, and Allah and his Messenger never said not to address hunger and thirst; they said to fulfill it in a legitimate way and to provide a legitimate way of doing that is the duty of the state. It is the case of this need, i.e., marriage. The state is bound to keep an eye on it and to have a check and balance because in different cultures it has been made too difficult sometimes from one side and sometimes on the side. Which has made it very difficult for people and they cannot fulfill those standards, due to not being able to fulfill those standards of getting married in the proper way it's hard to keep their chastity, morality, and peace. The Prophet said, "O assembly of youth! Whoever can afford to marry so he may marry, as this will lower the gaze and guard the private parts, and whoever cannot get married so he may fast as that is a shield [for his protection and chastity] (Bukhari and Muslim). Moreover, the Prophet said

> "Sultan" [ruler] is a guardian of one who does not have a guardian (Ahmad, Tirmizi)."

Also, the Prophet said

> "I am prior to the believers than their selves so whoever passed away and left a loan [due on him] so upon me is the payment and whoever left wealth, that is for his heirs (Bukhari and Muslim)".

This Hadith means that the *Khalifa* is the guardian, and one of the duties of the guardian is to arrange marriage for the people he handles.

The reason is very logical that humans want their desires to be fulfilled and for a Muslim that must be in a legitimate way. If people start fulfilling their desires in an illegitimate way, it will bring turmoil to the society ethically, socially, and politically. Because it proceeds towards conflicts, disputes, and bloodshed. While to maintain order and peace is the first ever duty of the state so it must think of the reasons and causes.

RIGHTS OF THE *KHALIFA*

As we have said that Islam as a perfect system describes the duties and rights of individuals, as well as institutions. Regarding the Khalifa, Ibn Jama'ah has mentioned ten fundamental rights of the Khalifa, as listed under:

1. OBEDIENCE TO THE *KHALIFA* WITH SINCERITY

As Allah said:

"Obey Allah and obey the Messenger and people in authority from amongst you" (4:59)

"People in authority from amongst you" means

(I) THEY MAY NOT BE OUTSIDERS; IN ISLAM, THERE IS NO ROOM FOR COLONIALISM.

(II) THEY MUST BE MUSLIMS

(III) THEY ARE MENTIONED AFTER OBEDIENCE TO ALLAH AND THE MESSENGER.

It means that as long as they do not order something against the Quran and Sunnah. There is no room for the obedience of any creature against Allah and his Messenger.

Allah said:

> *"And if you disputed in anything then take it back to Allah and the Messenger if you but believe in Allah and the last day- that is best and best as an interpretation (solution or as a result)." - (4:59)*

2. SINCERITY, LOOKING TOWARDS GOOD FOR THE *KHALIFA*:

The Prophet said,

> *"Deen is sincerity;", they said, "for whom?" The Prophet said, "For Allah, his Messenger, for Muslims in general and their leaders (Bukhari)."*

3. TO HELP HIM WHOLEHEARTEDLY

So, he may be able to protect the state and the public, to implement *Deen*, to control miscreants, and to counter invaders.

4. TO RESPECT HIM WELL AND WILLINGLY

As Khalifa is the agent of Allah, so he deserves respect. After the battle of the Trench when Sad Ibn Muaaz came riding on his donkey to decide and judge the case of Banu Quraizah the Prophet said, "Stand up for your chief."

5. TO ALERT HIM IF HE SHOWS ANY CARELESSNESS OR NEGLIGENCE.

The Prophet at the time of Hajj said in his sermon at Mina said,

> *"Three practices are there [if done] the heart of a believer will never get any malice [rust], sincere deeds*

for Allah, sincere advice to people in authority, and to be with the Jama'ah [of Muslims]."

6. TO INFORM AND WARN HIM OF INTERNAL AND EXTERNAL ENEMIES

This is because miscreants can conspire, so that must be countered. Otherwise, if he is not informed then there will be bloodshed or these bad people will gain control or the state may even disintegrate. Shah Wali Ullah said that to weaken and break the power of such people is a must.

7. TO HELP THE *KHALIFA* IN ANY POSSIBLE WAY

Because the *Khalifa* is looking after the state and public on behalf of the *Ummah*, so they are bound to help and support him to the best of their ability, so he may fulfill his duties with ease.

8. TO INFORM HIM ABOUT THE OFFICIALS OF THE STATE AND GOVERNMENT

To be aware of their good or bad qualities so he may encourage the good ones and warn or even remove the bad ones.

9. TO CONVINCE HIS OPPONENTS AND TO MAKE THEM INCLINED TO THE KHALIFA SO THAT THE *UMMAH* MAY BE UNITED AND UNIFIED.

Allah said:

"And obey Allah and his Messenger and dispute not lest you lose courage verily Allah is with the patient people."

10. TO DEFEND HIM WITH WORDS, ACTIONS, WEALTH, ET CETERA.

Because his disgrace is a disgrace to the state and the public and even to *Deen*.

As the Khalifa is devoted to this duty, so he may be given his needs and necessities in a reasonable way. When Abu Bakr became *Khalifa* the very next day, he was taking the cloaks, he went to the bazaar. Umar brought him to the masjid and told the Muslims that now he will be working for us, so we have to fulfill his needs.

Abu Bakr said you people know my business and manufacturing, which suffices for my family and me. However, now I will not be able to do that, so give me as much as a guardian and custodian of an orphan are given from the property of the orphans. Even though in his last moments, Abu Bakr ordered his son to sell his property. To pay back the whole amount he was given as salary to the exchequer.

These rights are the essential rights, depending on the situation and on what is needed for him as the fulfillment of his duties are concerned.

We want to mention here a few Ahadith of the Prophet:

1. The Prophet said:

    "Whoever obeyed me he obeyed Allah, and whoever disobeyed me, he has disobeyed Allah and whoever obeyed the Ameer *he obeyed me and whoever disobeyed the* Ameer *he disobeyed me" (Bukhari and Muslim).*

2. *"If a mutilated person has been made an* Ameer *upon you, and he leads you in accordance with the book of Allah then listen [to him] and obey" (Muslim).*

3. *"Listening and obedience is [must] for a man in what he liked and what he disliked as long as he has not*

been ordered to disobey [Allah and his Messenger] and who he has been ordered to disobey then there is no listening and no obedience." (Bukhari and Muslim)

DUTIES AND RESPONSIBILITIES OF THE CITIZEN

The general public, in both their individual and collective capacities, have duties that are binding, as they are citizens of the state. In this regard, we would like to say that the state must give the public a feeling that the state and government are their guardians, custodians, and servants who will protect them and their rights. Then for sure everyone will love the state and will fulfill their duties towards the state willingly. These duties are as follows:

A. TO ESTABLISH KHALAFAH

It means that people need someone to lead them, guide them, and shelter them, and that person is called the *Khalifa*, and as we said that the Khalifa represents Allah as his agent, so the actual source is Allah, but as a procedure he has to be appointed by the *ummah* in one way or the other. Islam has given the basic principles, but it has not given a specific framework, as Islam is a universal and everlasting religion. So, keeping in view the basic principles the people have to appoint their own *Khalifa*. That is the duty of *Ahlul Halli Wal Aqd*, to elect a *Khalifa*, and then the general public pledges their allegiance to him. In certain countries, even under the influence of western democracies, the public elects their representatives. Then those representatives elect the prime minister or the president, but in Islam the *Ahlul Halli Wal Aqd* elect the *Khalifa*, and the general public approves and ratifies this election. *Ahlul Halli Wal Aqd* are the learned, educated, experienced, and sincere leaders of the community. Therefore, their selection, election, or nomination will be the best way, because the general public neither knows the qualities nor understands the individual they are going to elect as a *Khalifa*. However, we can say that the people elect their leader because *Ahlul Halli Wal Aqd* represents them, and then the people approve their election by giving Bai'at to the Khalifa.

B. TO OBEY THE RULES AND LAWS

The pledge of allegiance means subjecting oneself to the laws of the land and these laws are the laws of Allah, and Allah said,

> *"Then nay they cannot be [considered] believers till they make you [O Muhammad!] A judge regarding what is disputed amongst them and then they do not find any resistance for what you have decreed and submit to it perfectly."*

Allah said:

> *"The saying of the believers when they are called to Allah and his Messenger to judge between them is that they say we heard, and we obeyed and such are the successful people." - (24:51)*

So, no one is allowed to take the law into his or her hands, as this creates turmoil and disorder. For the said purpose, there must be a judicial system free of any influence, and which has the executive power for the decree they have issued.

Umar wrote to Abu Musa Al-Ashlar that the judicial process is an established and mandatory practice. It must be followed and when someone has been appointed to it then know that to say a good word without its execution is meaningless.

C. TO ENJOIN GOOD AND FORBID EVIL

This is both the duty of the *Ummah* and the authority to enjoin good and forbid evil. Allah said:

> *"Let there be from amongst you a group calling towards good, enjoining good, forbidding evil and these are the successful people." - (3:104)*
>
> *"You are the best of people ever raised up for mankind, you promote good, prevent vice, and believe in Allah." - (3:110)*
>
> *"And for sure Allah will help one who helps him, indeed Allah is all strong, all-mighty. Those whom if we give them power in the land they will order for prayer and giving* Zakat, *enjoin good, forbid evil, and with Allah rest the end of matters."- (22:40,41)*

The state has the ability to do this, but the common people will do that as much as they can. This is the duty of each and every Muslim to the best of their ability.

To enjoin good does not have so many conditions, but to prevent evil has certain conditions, which will be listed under:

(I) THE PRACTICAL EXISTENCE OF EVIL:

So, one may not say to people not to do "such and such thing" which they are not doing at the time as this will make them curious about that.

(II) THAT EVIL IS DONE OPENLY:

Because common people are not allowed to chase and find out who is doing something wrong (i.e., vigilantes).

Allah said:

"And do not chase" (49:12).

Also, it can lead to suspicion for someone, which can be counter-productive.

Allah said:

"Avoid most of suspicion verily some suspicion is a [major] sin." - (49:12)

(III) TO STOP IT WITH THE EASIEST POSSIBLE MEANS:

One may not go to extremes, he may educate people about a certain thing, letting them know that you might not know, but this action is a forbidden act in Sharia. By doing so with kindness he will stop his wrongdoing.

Imam Ghazali, in his book *Keemya Sa'aadat*, mentioned these following ways:

(I) TO EDUCATE THE PERSON CONCERNED ABOUT THAT EVIL:

Maybe the person does not know that it is wrong, and that is why he is doing it.

(II)   TO CONVINCE HIM TO STOP IT:

Allah said,

> "Call to the path of your Lord with wisdom and with a nice advisory way" (16:125).

Hikmah, or wisdom means to speak in a suitable way, at an appropriate time, in an appropriate place.

(III) TO USE STRONG WORDS TO STOP HIM.

(IV) TO CHANGE THE ENVIRONMENT WITH HIS HANDS —

The Prophet said,

> "Whoever saw from amongst you evil, he may change it with his hand if he couldn't do that then with his tongue, and if he couldn't do that then he should hate it in his heart, and that is the weakest of Iman (faith)" (Muslim)

The Hadith means to change the evil with his hand in any possible way, then by the tongue, and then by heart. The scholars say, it depends on the situation and the power of the individual. While other scholars said that the first one is the duty of the people in authority, the second on is that of the scholars, and the third one is of the general public. However, we say that the Prophet used the word "whoever" which includes everyone, but it depends on the circumstances.

(V) TO WARN OF PUNISHMENT OR DEATH:

This is a strategy that is allowed for a broad-based good for the society.

(VI) TO PUNISH OR EVEN TO KILL:

This should be done with due process. Otherwise, it will cause a trouble immediately, and the after-effects could be worse than the crime that the person is being punished for.

(VII) TO ASK HELP OF OTHERS:

In this regard, a social boycott will be a good way.

To us, the best way is the department of *Hisbah* or ombudsman. This person has some power from the executive branch and some power from the judiciary branch as well, especially for emergencies. This means that the *ummah* is bound to help and support the *Khalifa* in his duties to keep an eye on wrongdoers and stop them as much as they can, provided that their way of stopping is not counterproductive.

(IV) TO OBTAIN KNOWLEDGE IN DIFFERENT FIELDS:

Societies are advancing rapidly through education. Especially nowadays, the entire world is like one global village. That is because of science and technology, and those who are superior in that field are the ones that are successful, and the rest are subject to them. Moreover, we know how much importance Islam has given to knowledge and education. That knowledge is of two types:

I. REGARDING THE GOOD LIFE OF THIS WORLD,

Allah said:

> *"Did you not see that Allah has subjugated to you all that is in the heaven and all that is in the earth and perfected on you his blessing [favors] open and hidden both."*

This term *Taskheer* used in the Holy Quran in dozens of places means that you have the talent to exploit it, and all these creatures have the ability to be exploited.

II. REGARDING THE PROSPEROUS LIFE IN THE HEREAFTER.

As humans have their physical side and spiritual as well, or they, have to have a relation with their creator and a relation with the creation. That is the characteristic of this special creature, i.e., the human.

Allah said:

> *"Then we originated him a different creature." - (23:14)*

> *"Indeed we have created humans in a beautiful stature." - (95:4)*

Moreover, the Prophet said:

> *"Indeed Allah created Adam in his shape."*

Some scholars said that "his shape" means the form of Allah, but Allah does not have any shape. As Allah is not a physical body, so again it means the shape that was his, meaning his most beloved shape.

Shah Wali Ullah said if a nation would have their *Deeni* (religious) side upright as far as the case of the hereafter is concerned, maybe they will have it good there. However, in this world they will be subject to others and would be enslaved. Which is against the very nature of *Tawheed* (belief in Allah and oneness), as it does not allow a human to be the slave of another in any way. That goes against the person's self-respect and dignity. If they are devoted to the benefit of this world only, they do not think of Allah. Alternatively, the hereafter where they will face the punishment, while the true Muslim has to think of his good here in this world and the hereafter, so in each and every field they must have the education to support the state and the *Khalifa*. Such a society will be a balanced society.

(VIII) TO WORK FOR THEIR LIVELIHOOD:

It is the duty of every individual not to be a burden on others or society.

Allah said:

> *"Allah puts forward the example of an owned slave having no power over anything and a man whom we have given good provision, so he spent there from secretly and openly (with free will), can they be equal? All praises be to Allah but of them know not.*
>
> *And Allah puts forward an example of two men one of them is mute [and deaf] having no power over anything and he is a burden to his master wherever he directs him he can bring no good, is such a man equal to one who orders justice [and he can implement it] and he is on the straight path." - (16:75-76).*

So, one who earns his livelihood is not a burden to the society; rather, he contributes in one way or the other. So, where there is no hunger, and where basic needs are fulfilled, for sure there will be peace and justice within that society. As we mentioned before that the two fundamental pillars of a welfare state are:

(I) FULFILLMENT OF BASIC NEEDS AND NECESSITIES.

(II) PEACE AND NO FEAR.

Moreover, as we mentioned before, these two are inter-connected. Shah Wali Ullah said that the state has to encourage physical labor like the agriculture, industry, and business as this provides jobs and produces revenue. The economic stability of a state provides a field for further good.

Shah Abdul Qadir said,

> *"Character comes from the situation not only from education."*

Even Adam Smith said that humanity is influenced by their faith and economic conditions, and whenever there is a conflict of both of these, economic conditions prevail and overtakes, and the people go for that.

Qazi Abu Yusuf also wrote in his book "Kitab Ul Kharaj" that people might be provided incentives so they may work whole-heartedly.

Shah Wali Ullah said that farmers should be given such support that no piece of land remains barren and uncultivated. Traders (i.e., merchants and businesspeople) may be offered incentives so they may bring beneficial things from all around, and they will also compete for quality and price.

(IX) SOCIAL RESPONSIBILITY –

As a state is one entity and people and institutions are its part and organs, and they depend upon one another, so they have to cooperate, help, and support each other. They also have to help those who are in need.

> *The Prophet said, "The Muslims in their relation to one another, their leniency towards one another, is*

> *like one body: when a part of it feels sick, the whole body feels sick."*

For the said purpose Islam has imposed *Zakat* on those who have the equal of Nisab i.e., a specific amount of savings at the end of the year, in order to give 2.5% of that to the poor. Also, there are certain other responsibilities, even though these are ethical and moral but Islam gives priority to ethics over laws and rules.

Imam Bukhari narrated a Hadith from Abu Saeed wherein the Prophet said that whoever has any extra food, he should give it to one who does not have it; whoever has an extra mount (traditionally a camel, horse, donkey, etc. but now perhaps a car or other motor vehicle) he should give it to one who does not have it; then he mentioned a few types of belongings that we thought that on one has any (undisputed) right in extra.

Now if the rich do not give from the wealth they have on their own, then the general public may convince them and even the state under the doctrine of necessity can make some law in this regard.

In a Hadith Qudsi,

Allah said,

> *"Rich people are my agents and the poor are my family, so when my agents will become miserly towards my family, I will cause them to taste my punishment, and I don't care."*

Hafiz Ibn Hazm said

> *The rich are bound to take care of the poor, and he said, this is unanimously agreed upon issue amongst the scholars (Al Muhalla).*

Imam Mawardi said

> *When the Khalifa fulfilled his duties to Allah then the ummah is bound to do two things toward him, obedience and help.*

That is why Ibn Khaldun said; that the characteristic of *Khalafah* is that it takes care of the good of the people in this world and the hereafter.

As an objective, the hereafter is the first and most important thing but as we exist in this world, this world comes first, and this is the way toward the hereafter, so it is must to be better in this world as well. That is why Allah said:

> *"Indeed we sent our messengers with clear rules, and we sent down with them the scriptures and the scale (balanced system) so that mankind may stand with justice." - (57:25)*

(X) JIHAD –

This is another duty of the Ummah towards the state to do "Jihad."

"Jihad" comes from the root word *Jah'd* or *Juh'd* which means striving hard. We can apply this word to any effort, which is for some good cause in any way, or that is a duty even, and he fulfills that. Even the Holy Quran has used this for other than fighting as well because fighting was ordered after migration. However, still the law of Jihad is found there in Makki Surahs while there was no fight ordered, but instead of retaliation the Muslims were ordered to be patience and had stability.

Allah said:

> "So obey not the disbelievers and do Jihad with them by this [Quran] the great Jihad" (25:52).

It means to call them and convince them with this Quran.

Abu Zar relates that the Prophet said, "The best Jihad is to strive hard against oneself and one's desires."

In Hajj, someone asked the Prophet about the best Jihad, and he said the best Jihad is to speak out against a tyrant ruler.

However, Jihad in the meaning of fighting is the "hump: of Islam. A hump increases the beauty and the price of a camel or a bull, and that is the highest part of their body and clearly seen. Thus, the Prophet said to Muaaz that Jihad is the hump of Islam (Tirmizi).

However, each and every order of Allah either has a time fixed for it like prayer and fasting, or the situation is mentioned. For Jihad there is a necessary situation,

the Prophet said,

> "Don't wish for facing the enemy but when you face them, then be stable."

So, Jihad has its prerequisites, and when these occur then, Jihad becomes incumbent upon Muslims.

Reasons for Jihad: as the name of Allah is "Momin" and belief in Allah and his message is called Iman while one who accepted his message is called Muslim, and the religion is called Islam. Now Islam means "to avail peace and to provide it." A Muslim is the one who avails and provides it.

Iman means to avail and provides security and "Momin" means the one who provided security. Now all these term roam around peace and security, so if we start with a *Deen* whose concepts starts with peace and security, then how can it encourage something opposite to that? But when it does go for that, it means that the situation has gone to adverse. And that's why all the four schools of jurisprudence said that the cause of Jihad in the meaning of fight is to bring the situation back to the original status. Which is peace, but peace is at stake, and a big and disastrous situation is on the doorstep and there is a fear of bloodshed so it must be averted. This concept is clearly mentioned in the Holy Quran. Allah said:

> *"And fight them until there is no* Fitnah *[remaining]"* (2:193)

Then Allah said:

> *"And if they cease then there is no transgression [retaliation] but against the wrongdoers."*

In chapter 8:38, after a similar order Allah said:

> *"Then if they cease then for sure Allah is the watcher of what they do." - (8:38)*

It means that if they cease, and you felt it in one way or the other, then go ahead and accept their seizure and if they cheat then Allah is watching them. This is just like the verse of "Silm" (reconciliation and peace treaty). Allah said:

> *"And if they [the enemies on the battlefield] are inclined to peace, then you may incline to it [as well] and put trust in Allah- verily he is the all-hearer, the all-knower." - (8:61)*

This means if there is enmity and fighting with each other, then when they ask for peace, for sure you will have reservations that it is simply a ruse and they are preparing themselves to attack once again.

But this is the life of this world, where things do not stand still and are not the same forever; neither peace nor war go on forever, rather things come and go. You must be alert, well prepared, and aware of the situation in order to make correct decisions. While war is inevitable and the idea of peace can be accepted, if they are inclined to it whole-heartedly then accept it and put your trust in Allah. Because as humans we are living in this world with others. We are social by nature, and we need each other, Muslims, and non-Muslims alike, so we need to think of that and decide accordingly.

So basically, the Muslim state has to be well prepared for any situation that it might face, and that is why Allah said before the previous verse mentioned above:

> *"And make ready against them all you can of power including steeds of war to threaten the enemy of Allah and your enemy and others besides them who you do not know." - (8:60)*

Allah did not say to kill them or even to fight them; rather He says to threaten them with weapons and preparations. Which, in other words, means to control their conspiracies and threats of war, so we can say that there must be deterrents available to maintain peace. But if war breaks out, and then the enemy shows that they are inclined to peace, Muslims may incline to that as well. It means that they started the war, and you retaliated, but still when they turned to peace then that is the original concept, so you may turn to it also. But when is war inevitable and unavoidable?

When we look into the Holy Quran and teachings of the Prophet, we do not find that people may be fought because they are non-Muslims or disbelievers in Islam. Or the Muslims, when they are fighting Muslims, may never be fought. It does not matter how dangerous they are to public safety. It might be the other way around, that sometimes the Muslims are fought and other times the non-Muslims are safe and protected. It means that the cause and reason for fighting are not lack of faith or being non-Muslim. Rather, the cause is *Harabah* which means that they either started a war, so the Muslims have a duty to defend, counter, and retaliate, or they are plotting against Islam and Muslims or the Muslim state so again Muslims are duty-bound to counter that and to defuse it. This is not only a right but a duty as we know that the army and its soldiers are bound to fight and defend. If they do not do so, they might be charged and punished by court martial.

The Holy Quran said:

> *(I) "Indeed Allah defends those who believed and Allah does not like any treachery, ungratefulness. Permission to fight is given to those [believers] who are being fought [war is imposed on them] because they have been wronged, and Allah can help them. Those [believers] who have been expelled from their homes unjustly [without any just reason] but only that they say, "our Lord is Allah."*
> *- (22:38)*

In these verses, Allah has mentioned that

(I) WAR HAS BEEN IMPOSED ON THEM, AND MANY INJUSTICES HAVE BEEN DONE TO THEM.

(II) THEY HAVE BEEN TURNED OUT OF THEIR HOMES ONLY BECAUSE OF THEIR FAITH, AND FAITH IS A MATTER OF FREE WILL AND NOT A CRIME.

So, one may not be driven out for that, and nor should his property be taken.

> *(II) "And what is wrong with you who fight not in the cause of Allah and for those oppressed among men, women,*

and children, who cry our Lord! Take us out of this city of oppressive people and provide us from your side a protector and provide us from your side a helper." - (4:75)

(III)   *"And fight in the path of Allah those who fight you, and transgress not the limits. Verily Allah does not like the transgressors." - (2:19)*

In this verse, Allah says to fight those who fight you. Meaning, they have imposed the fight and now you are bound to counter that, and if you do not, then that is a sin. But still the rule is not to transgress the limits and not to exceed in retaliation. While, in the verse, as we mentioned before, helpless, and weak people are being oppressed. They are crying for help, and if you can help them, then why would you not?

(IV)   *"And fight them until there is no* fitnah *[remaining]." - (2:193)*

Fitnah is a word or term used for different meanings. It depends on the situation, so conspiracy is a *fitnah*, weakening the Islamic state is a *fitnah*. Usurping the Islamic state's property or rights is a *fitnah*. All these are wrong and are a form of cruelty, and any harm or cruelty must be countered. If not, it will engulf the state and then it will not be easy to defend the state, its sovereignty, or its resources. But as soon as the *fitnah* ceases, then you may not proceed further.

(V)   *"Then whoever has assaulted you, assault him the way he assaulted you and fear Allah and know that Allah is with the* Muttaqeen*. - (2:194)*

The word *Muttaqeen* literally means "those who avoid" and they are very careful regarding their actions. They do not lose their temper or self-control even in extraordinary circumstances, and they do not retaliate disproportionately either.

Keeping in view all these verses we come to know that the cause of fighting is

(A) THE OTHER SIDE HAS IMPOSED WAR, SO THEY HAVE TO ADDRESS THE ISSUE.

(B) THERE IS *FITNAH*, SO THEY HAVE TO TAKE PRECAUTIONS AND TO CONTROL IT BEFORE A BIG TRAGEDY OCCURS.

> (III) PEOPLE HAVE BEEN TURNED OUT OF THEIR HOMES BECAUSE OF THEIR FAITH AND BELIEFS, SO THEY HAVE NOT JUST THE RIGHT BUT THE DUTY TO RECAPTURE THEIR PROPERTY.

> (III) PEOPLE ARE UNJUSTLY OPPRESSED, AND THE WEAK ARE CRYING FOR HELP.

So, you may assist them with the easiest possible means. Even though the verse is applied to the case of the Muslims primarily, if the non-Muslims are being oppressed unjustly, and they ask for help, and it is possible to help, it is good to do so. Especially when the state has a treaty with their nation.

The Prophet supported his non-Muslim allies when they came to the Prophet and cried for help. The case of the Khuza'ah tribe is a good example. They were the allies of Abdul - Muttalib from the times of ignorance, and the Prophet used to honor that treaty. But when Khuza'ah and Banu-Bakr fought, and Quraish helped Banu-Bakr against Khuza'ah while they were subject to the treaty of Hudaibiyah, they broke the treaty. And Khuza'ah asked for help from the Prophet, and that became the basis and reason for the conquest of Makah.

Now all these reasons mentioned in these verses are when fighting is inevitable and becomes incumbent upon Muslims, it could be confined to *Harabah*, oppression, and *Fitnah*, and nobody can make any reservation or have an objection because this is a logical and reasonable method, and the whole world has done that in their respectable times and still they do so. Even regarding Muslims if they do injustice, fighting them is a must.

Also, Allah said:

> *"And if two groups amongst the believers fall into fight, then make peace between them both, but if one of them rebels against the other then fight you [all] against that one who rebels till it complies with the command of Allah, then if it complies then make reconciliation between them justly"* (49:9)

Now here both groups are Muslims but the other Muslims may fight the rebellious group. So, in brief we say that Islam believes in *Dawat* and to promote good and forbid evil and to establish peace. But when a situation occurs, and fighting becomes inevitable, then no excuse can be made. When it started, then it may be taken to its natural end, which is either to cut off the power from the miscreants or to make them surrender and submit, or at least consider, peace.

RIGHTS OF THE CITIZENS

As we said, rights and duties are interlinked, so we mentioned the responsibilities of the *Khalifa* and then his rights. Then we mentioned the obligations of the citizen, and now we have to mention the rights of the citizen. Purposely we mentioned the duties first in both cases because of the covetousness; most people are always talking about rights but never mention the responsibilities. Obligations on one side safeguard the rights of the other, as the duties of the one hand are the rights for the other side, directly or indirectly. Here we will discuss the rights of the citizens. These are called fundamental rights, essential rights, or human rights. When these rights are violated, then it creates turmoil within in the state. *Haqq*, or right, does not originate from nature, but in Islam the source of every *Haqq* is the entity of Allah. As Allah has given the same right so, no one can take it from anyone for no particular reason. One can exercise one's rights as long as it does not harm others. So, it brings two bonds:

(I) Everyone must respect and honor the rights of others.

(II) One who exercises his right may not harm another. Then there are:

A. THE RIGHTS OF ALLAH AND THESE ARE THE DUTIES OF PEOPLE

It includes belief in Allah and His *Deen* and obedience to the commandments of his *Deen*.

B. THE RIGHTS OF PEOPLE.

The type of rights can be of a person or humanity in general. In the case of personal rights, the person concerned can forgive, pardon, and drop it.

C. RIGHTS THAT CONTAIN BOTH CONCEPTS,

i.e., the right of Allah and the rights of people. But if the notion of the right of Allah is prevailing in it then it is annexed to the first type. If the concept is the right of a human, then it could be pardoned.

Our topic here is human rights, so let us examine what human rights are. Life exists because it survives. It survives the ravages of transgression by homologous and heterologous competitors (not Darwinism, but similar). We humans live in a highly advanced sociopolitical organization, so society must honor the rights of one another.

Human rights are of two types:

1. PUBLIC RIGHTS

e.g., maintaining peace and not to harming things related to the public.

2. PRIVATE RIGHTS

These are the personal rights of an individual. These rights cannot be abolished nor taken away.

Some essential rights are listed under:

A. IN ISLAM, FIVE THINGS ARE VERY VALUABLE AND PRECIOUS, AND THESE ARE:

(I) LIFE -

No one can take the life of another, as life is sacred and secured by the laws of Allah. For the said protection, Islam has the law of retribution. Allah said: "and for you in retribution there is life, O people of understanding, so you may be protected [or you may avoid killing]." This is the case of intentional murder, while in the event of an accidental death restitution (blood money) is to be paid to the family.

(II) PROPERTY –

No one can take or damage the property of another, and if someone does, then s/he will be liable for damages.

(III) FAITH AND RELIGION –

Whatever the faith of someone is, no one can harm him because of their beliefs. In Islam, there is the concept of *Zimmah* and a *Zimmi*; the non-Muslim citizens of an Islamic state have full protection, the same as a Muslim. As Islam says to leave them alone with their religion. Also, it says for them is what is for us and upon them is what is on us.

(IV) HONOR –

Allah said:

> "And indeed we have honored the children of Adam" (17:70).

So, Allah gives this honor to all people so no one can harm anyone in his honor.

(V) KNOWLEDGE AND INTELLECT –

This is another valuable and protected right of an individual. No one can either harm another physically, like getting someone addicted to drugs, nor can anyone poison the thinking of another. Even to force someone to change their beliefs is not permissible; one can only inform the person about the truth and let him or her think about it.

B. RIGHT OF FREEDOM

the primary motto of Islam is "there is no god but Allah", meaning there is no slavery to anybody except to the creator and real Lord. That is why Umar said to his governor, "people were delivered by their mothers as free people, since when did you think they are slaves?" And Ribai, Ibn Aamar said to the Persian authority, "Allah has appointed us to bring humans out of the slavery of humans and make them the slaves of the Lord of humans."

C. THE RIGHT TO ACQUIRE BASIC NEEDS

as we said, Islam does not forbid people from fulfilling their natural needs, it only specifies that it should be done in a legitimate way. Also, Islam persuades and encourages people to work and earn and never to be a burden on others. The person must try to earn and give to others and not to beg, take, or expect from others.

D. THE RIGHT OF OWNERSHIP AND POSSESSION

When earning is allowed or even encouraged, then it is logical to keep, owns, and possesses one's earnings and the things one can purchase with them. And as we mentioned that property is one of the five valuable things and no one can harm another's property. So many rights arise from this concept of property ownership and possession. The Prophet of Allah said, "Whoever is killed defending his property is martyred." This right goes to both men and women of any age and even applies to babies and unborn children in the womb, in certain cases like wills or inheritance. Allah said:

> *"Eat up not the properties of each other unjustly" (2:188).*

Also, Allah said:

> *"But if that is a trade by mutual consent" (4:28)*

E. THE RIGHT TO EDUCATION

Humans have reason intellect; they need education and can acquire it. So, nobody can be deprived of this right as well because education is not a privilege but a right. Allah has commanded us to read and learn; even the revelation to the Prophet started with this order.

> *"Read in the name of your Lord who created. Who created humanity from the clot. Read and your Lord is the respect, giver. The one who taught with the pen. Who taught humanity what he did not know (before)"*

So, Allah mentioned,

(I) TO READ,

(II) TO READ IN HIS NAME,

(III) HE HAS CREATED THE WHOLE WORLD,

(IV) HE CREATED HUMANS FROM A CLOT,

(V) READ,

(VI) YOUR LORD IS THE RESPECT GIVER,

(VII) HE TAUGHT WITH THE PEN,

(VIII) HE TAUGHT WHAT HUMANS DID NOT KNOW.

It means that a person may study *Deen* and the world as well, as Allah mentioned reading in his name, then said the creation of the whole world, and then the creation of humans. He repeated the order to show the importance of education and knowledge. He mentioned the method of obtaining education i.e., the pen. How small a pen is, but how much greatness can one achieve with it, because humanity has reason and intellect, and people can utilize little things to significant purpose. Also, Allah said that he taught people what they did not know before. Which means this is a continuous process until the Day of Judgment and as humans have two aspects of their life. So, they are in needs of two types of education:

(I) THE RELIGIOUS TYPE,

(II) WORLDLY KNOWLEDGE AND HOW TO USE THE THINGS IN THIS WORLD.

F. THE RIGHT OF EXPRESSION/FREEDOM OF THOUGHT AND FREEDOM OF SPEECH

Speaking and expression is also natural for humans as Allah said:

> "The most Beneficent, he taught the Holy Quran, He created people and taught him how to speak and express." - (55:1-4)

> "Then by the Lord of the heaven and the earth, this [message/Quran/ life after death] is as accurate as you speak." (51:23)

Implicitly this verse says that speech is a reality. So, everyone has the right to speak his mind, but with only on the condition that it is not harmful to others and does not corrupt social values or ethics. But there are some exceptions. Allah said:

> *"Allah does not like to speak evil loud but one who has been wronged." - (4:148)*

Sometimes in retaliation someone says a similarly harsh word, which can be an excuse for him.

G. THE RIGHT OF CONSCIOUSNESS / RIGHT OF RELIGIOUS CONVICTION

All humans believe in something. Sometimes that is in a divine concept while other times it is a created concept, and that created concept is called religion. The relation of every person to their *Deen* and religion is in such a way that they cannot tolerate any challenge or criticism to it. They become angry, lose their temper, and retaliate. That's why even if religion is based on a wrong concept; still it may not be condemned in a challenging way as it is counterproductive. Allah said:

> *"And do not revile [insult, vilify] those who invoke others besides Allah, otherwise they will revile Allah spitefully in ignorance. Thus, we have made the actions of all men seem pleasing." - (6:108)*

This verse means neither reviles the worshippers nor their gods. Also,

Allah said:

> *For every nation, we have appointed rituals that they observe, so let them not dispute with you on the matter." - (22:69)*

Yes, debate with arguments to educate people about *Deen*, and to distinguish the right from wrong, is the duty of the Messenger and his followers. But it may be in a nice and proper way to convince others to accept the truth. Allah said:

> *"Requite evil with good." (41:34)*

> *"And have disputes with them in the best manner." - (16:125)*

It means that *Deen* is a matter of free will. That is why Islam does not allow converting someone by force. Allah said:

> *"There is no coercion in the matter of faith; indeed, guidance has become clear from misguidance, so whoever believes in* Taghut *[wrong concept of God and religion] and believes in Allah has firmly held the strong hand hold [of the rope of Allah]." - (2:256)*

> *"And whoever wills let him disbelieve and whoever wills let him believe." - (18:29)*

Yes, the ultimate end is with Allah, and everyone would be put to accountability on the Day of Judgment for his faith and character.

H. THE RIGHT OF FREE MOVEMENTS AND MIGRATION

People are a living and mobile entity, and they are bound to look and think for their benefit. For the said purpose, they need freedom of movement.

Allah said:

> *"Have they not travelled in the land" (12:109, 22:46, 40:82)*

"So travel in the land" - *(3:137,16:36)*

There are so many other verses that call for a free movement, both explicitly and implicitly.

Yes, the purpose could be different; some will travel for seeking knowledge while some others for jobs, business, and even entertainment. Yes, their travel and movement may not be in an illegal way or for some illegal things, but imposing restrictions does not mean that one has no right to free movement. Even Allah mentioned free movement for trade as a favor for the people of Makah, i.e., the Quraish as he said,

> *"Because of taming the Quraish, their timing of the trips of winter and summer, they may worship the Lord of the house." - (106:1-3)*

I. THE RIGHTS OF ASSOCIATION

as humans are social by nature, they cannot live in isolation, and that is why solitary confinement should not be legal anywhere under normal circumstances. So, everyone should be allowed live in society to take part in social activities and in the concept of *Jama'ah* which is so important in Islam.

HUMANS ARE CONSIDERED AS KHALIFA, AND KHALAFAH IS OF TWO TYPES;

(I) THE OBVIOUS ONE,

(II) THE NONOBVIOUS.

And this second one is to be in a bond, subject to some authority and rule and to preserve and protect his due rights as well. This party could be a social one or a political one. That is logical, reasonable, and needed. Because everyone does not know everything, we all need to consult someone or seek advice, and this creates a link in one way or the other. The concept of *Shura* is imperative in Islam, and that produces the concept of groups.

J. THE RIGHT OF JUSTICE

There is no peace without justice, as peace is needed, so justice is essential.

Allah said:

> "Say (O Muhammad) my Lord has commanded justice." - (7:29)

> "Indeed Allah commands justice and kindness." - (16:9)

> "O you who believe! Be firm in establishing justice." - (4:135)

> "O you who believe! Stand out firmly for Allah and be a just witness, and let not the enmity to others make you avoid justice, be just that is nearer to piety." - (5:8)

It means that justice is a must, even in the case of an enemy. Even if your enemies have done wrong to you in *Deen*, if they prevented and stopped you from the house of Allah to perform worship still you are bound to do justice. It may not be taken towards injustice. Allah said:

> "And let not your enmity to a nation that they have stopped you from "Al Masjid Ul Haram" [Holy Kaba] may not lead you to transgression." - (5:2)

K. THE RIGHT OF PROTEST

if some wrong is done to someone, even though forgiveness and not retaliating is appreciated and welcomed, sometimes it does not work, so retaliation is allowed. Allah said when he praises those who have a strong and firm belief and trust in Allah, and he mentioned some of their qualities:

> *"And those who when an oppressive wrong is done to them they take revenge, the recompense for an evil is evil like thereof...." - (42:39)*

So, if revenge is allowed, then to speak against an evil being done to one is also not only allowed, but rather it is one's right. Abu Bakr, the first successor of the Prophet, said in his first address that

> *"Cooperate as long as I am in the right direction and correct me when I make a mistake." While the second successor said, "If I deviate from the right path, what will you people do?"*

Then one Bedouin jumped up and said that

> *"We will straighten your crookedness with the edge of our swords."*

After that, Umar came to him and embraced him and thanked Allah that he has created such people who would straighten him if he deviated. All these rights are the duties of the state so it may preserve and protect this for each and every citizen.

MORE THAN ONE *KHALIFA*

Islam, in its very motto of *Tawheed*, insisted upon unity and unification as Allah said:

> *"And hold fast all of you together to the rope of Allah and be not divided among yourselves." - (3:103)*

> *"And obey Allah and his Messenger and do not dispute lest you lose courage and your strength depart and be patient (stable and steadfast)." - (8:46)*

> *"Indeed those who divided their* Deen *and they were in sects you (O Muhammad) are not from them in any way." - (6:159)*

It means that you have nothing to do with them as they are divided. Moreover, you are for unity, *Tawheed* asks for unity and division goes towards *Shirk* (polytheism).

> *"And be not from the polytheists, those who split up then religion and became sects." - (30:31-32)*

It means implicitly that the Muslims may have only one *Khalifa* and they are united under his *Khalafah*. The division produces hatred jealousy, greed, and enmity. Also, that is not only harmful to their power but their *Deen* as well.

Now as long as *Deen* was strong and people were pious then the entire *ummah* had only one *Khalifa*. However, as much as *Deen* is becoming weak in people, they are divided, and the result is a loss of their power, authority, honor, and dignity. Now basically the whole ummah agrees that the Muslims must have only one Khalifa but according to Karramiyyah, it is ok to have two *Khalifas* or more in different regions. He said that Ali was a *Khalifa* and Muawiya was another *Khalifa* at the same time, and none of Ahlul Sunnah ever said that either of them was a sinner or a criminal. Yes, at most one can say that Muawiya was in an analogical error, which is not a sin. Both of them had companions of the Prophet and major followers with them.

Khateeb also said the same: it is also said in "Al Mawafiq" (a book) if one *Khalifa* can take care of the whole area then the concept of two is wrong. If not because the area is too l then that is ok to have two *Khalifas* according to some scholars.

Imam Nawawi said in his commentary on Saheeh Muslim that having two Imams is wrong, and this is an issue agreed upon by the *ummah*.

Allama Mawardi said, if both got *Bai'at* at the same time then both are void. If they got it one after the other then the first one is valid and the second is void. However, if it is unknown who got it first, then some scholars said both are void, while others said there should be a draw between them and if both are done at the same time but with one *Bai'at* then both are void as well (Abu Yala).

Shafiites say that to have two Imams is not allowed as this is against the very spirit of unity, which is the order of Allah (Mughnil Muhtaj). For them, if the second Imam got the *Bai'at*, and it was known to him that already a *Khalifa* has been appointed for the *ummah*, then this second Imam may be punished.

Arfajah Al Ash'jaee said that the Prophet said.

"Whosoever came to you, and you were united upon one, and he [the newcomer] was trying to split your stick or to break your Unity, then kill him." (Muslim)

However, when Muslims have many areas in their control, and it is difficult for one *Khalifa* to take care of them, it should be permissible to have more than one *Khalifa*. We say in different areas they should have their ruler but, in some way, they should be united under a central leadership of a *Khalifa*, as it was the case in "Khalafah Uthmaniyyah", even though that is a symbolic one.

THE CHARACTERISTICS OF THE ISLAMIC SYSTEM

1. ALLAH IS THE RULER AND QURAN AND SUNNAH ARE THE SUPREME LAW -

As we said that Allah is the sole creator of the whole world and humans as well. Allah is the Lord, and he has given fundamental principles to humans on how to act and practice to make their life a good one here and a prosperous one in the hereafter. The very creator and Lord, who knows all about the past, present, and future, gave this system. Therefore, Allah knows the qualities and capabilities of humans and their faults and shortcomings also. So only his system can qualify their needs and necessities and can give them the good here in this world and the hereafter.

Allah has comprehensive knowledge, inclusive mercy, irresistible power, and is never affected by anything, be it a situation, power, or person. Moreover, he sent the Prophet Muhammad as the last Prophet to the whole world to ensure the system he has given will be the perfect one, qualifying each and every time and for each and every situation. So, this system gave us principles, and it has left a vast field of the deduction for the jurists according to different circumstances.

So, this system has one part known as "Sharia" where the laws are clearly mentioned in the text of Quran and Sunnah. There is no room for the use of reason, or intellect and no room for deduction. The other part is known as *Fiqh*, and these are the laws deduced by the authentic jurists by the situations they faced. These are changeable if needed but may be replaced with similar laws deduced by the authentic jurists in the framework of the well-known rules of deduction.

Regarding the first category Allah said:

> *"It is not for a believing man or a believing woman when Allah and his Messenger have decreed a matter that they should have any option in their [own] affair [even] and whoever will disobey Allah and his Messenger he has indeed strayed in a plain error." - (33:36)*

Regarding the second one Allah said:

> *"And if you differ in anything amongst yourselves then refer it to Allah and his Messenger if you believe in Allah and the last day. That is better and more suitable for final determination." - (4:59)*

Also, Allah said:

> *"And if they would have referred it to the Messenger or those in charge of authority [knowledge] among them than those who could deduce from amongst them would have understood it." - (4:83)*

2. THE RELATION OF INDIVIDUALS AMONGST THEM AND WITH THE STATE AND SOCIETY -

In a society based on an Islamic system, the line is drawn and clearly stipulated to what extent an individual can go for his sake. Also, when the state or society can interfere in the matters of individuals, Islam has given the right of work, ownership, and possession. This inspires the individual to try and strive hard. However, they are not to harm the society or its public and social rights, but rather to support it as both, depend upon each other. People are social by nature so a healthy society can assure his safety, honor, and dignity, so he has to give to the society, and the society will give back to him as well.

Allah said:

> *"And seek in that which Allah has given you the Hereafter and do not forget your portion from the world." - (28:77)*

In Islam, the society is one unit and like one body, while individuals are its parts. If a part of the body suffers, it causes pain to the whole body. Moreover, if the ailment becomes chronic and untreatable, then it will eventually cause death to the body.

3. THE RULERS ARE FROM THE UMMAH -

As Allah said:

> *"O you who believe! Obey Allah and obey the Messenger and those in authority from amongst you." - (4:59)*

This *ayah* means Islam does not allow colonialism because that is a type of slavery. That is against the very honor and dignity of the individual and nation as well, while the pledge of allegiance in Islam means no to the slavery of all except Allah alone.

4. ETHICAL AND MORAL EDUCATION OF THE NATION

As we know, man-made laws to deal with worldly and physical affairs. These laws have nothing to do with spirituality, ethics, or morality, while people by nature have animal characteristics. They have lust and anger, and when lust and anger combine and are supported by intellect, the result is disorder, mischief, and bloodshed. This lust and anger are both natural, but if it has not been polished, civilized, and cultured, then the result is disastrous and dangerous. That is why its correction and polishing is a must, and that is possible through education and nourishment. An ethical society can never be corrupt either in its political process nor its economic and financial one. These three are connected to each other and depend on one another. For thirteen years, the Prophet made people ethically correct, and when they migrated to Medina, the state that was run by these individuals was an exemplary state.

The Prophet said,

"I have been sent to perfect noble character."

A man of character does not do wrong, and if it happened, he repents and admits that he has done wrong. He apologizes, asks for forgiveness, pays the damages, and presents himself for accountability.

5. GOVERNMENT BY THE WILL OF PEOPLE BUT WITH CONDITIONS

In today's democracies, the government is that of the will of the general public. Those who are elected by the public have the freedom to make or remove any law. However, in Islam those who nominate or elect the *Khalifa* are people of known qualities. The *Khalifa* must have the required qualities; the *Ahlul Shura* must have the right qualities, which we have mentioned already. Yes, in the west and east this concept of conditions, qualities, and restrictions are common, but these conditions, qualities, and restrictions differ from country to country, region to region, and culture to culture. Democracy does not have a universal form. An individual who is not a citizen cannot usually run for elected office. One who has a felony on his record does not have the right to vote. Moreover, one who is not a citizen of the United States by birth cannot contest for the presidency. In such a way, Islam has its conditions, requirements, and restrictions. So, the Parliament with all its supremacy cannot make any law against the Quran and Sunnah. Because the actual sovereignty and rule belongs to Allah, so the parliament or the *Khalifa* is sovereign but for some limits and bounds.

THE CHARACTERISTICS OF

THE ISLAMIC STATE

An Islamic state is a particular form of nation; it has certain characteristics:

I. IN AN ISLAMIC STATE THE SUPREMACY AND SOVEREIGNTY BELONG TO ALLAH AND ALLAH IS THE LORD AND THE RULER,

As Allah said:

   i. "Rule is but for Allah [alone]." - (6:57, 12:40 and 67)

   ii. "Beware! to him [Allah] belongs the rule." - (6:62)

   iii. "Beware! to him belongs the creation and the rule." - (7:54)

This last verse mentioned the reason also that when Allah is the creator then he is to be the ruler as well.

Allah said:

> *"And he does not make anyone like his partner in his rule." - (18:26)*

The rulers in an Islamic state are his agents only, as Allah said:

> *"And He [Allah] is the one who made you agents on the earth." - (6:165)*

> *"Then we made you agents on earth, so we may see how you would work." - (10:14)*

So, the *Khalifa* or the ruler does not have the real supremacy. That is for Allah alone. All his acts must be in accordance with the Quran and Sunnah, otherwise it will be null and void.

II. QURAN AND SUNNAH ARE THE SUPREME LAW OF ANY ISLAMIC STATE

so, parliament cannot make any law against it. Even where any law is going to be made, that must be by the authentic jurist by the known procedure of deduction, Allah said in many verses:

"Obey Allah and obey the Messenger."

III. THE *KHALAFAH* AND THE STRUCTURE OF THE STATE AND AUTHORITY MAY BE BY THE CONSENT OF THE PEOPLE

As the *Khalifa* is to be nominated and elected by their elders. They are called *Ahlul Halli Wal Aqd* dually consented to by the general public in one way or the other as we stated. Moreover, if the whole *Ummah* or the majority goes against Sharia, it does not have any legitimacy.

IV. THE WHOLE *UMMAH* MAY BE UNITED ON THE BASIS OF *DEEN* AS THE FUNDAMENTAL LAW OF THAT STATE

Because in such a state the status of tribe, clan, color, culture, and geography is secondary.

Allah said:

> *"And hold the rope of Allah together [as a whole] and be not divided." - (3:103)*

Yes, the non-Muslim citizens in such a state are considered non-Muslim faith-wise, but they are constitutional Muslims as they submit to Islam as the law of the land and as the constitution. This concept does not allow any room for any discrimination, and the Prophet made it clear in his sermon, but even the Holy Quran itself when it said,

> *"O Mankind! Indeed, We created you from one male and one female." - (49:13)*

> *"O Mankind! Be dutiful to your Lord the one who created you [all] from one soul [Adam] and who created from that [soul] his wife [Eve] and he created from them both many men and women." - (4:1)*

This means that all are equal.

V. THE VIRTUE IN SUCH A STATE IS TO HAVE PIETY, HONESTY, TRUTHFULNESS, AND NOBLE CHARACTER.

So, this state is a welfare state, taking care of everyone, provides justice and treats people kindly, fulfills its obligations, even towards the visitors and even other non-Muslims.

Allah said:

> *"Fear Allah and be with the truthful people." (9:119)*

"Fear Allah and speak the truth [to the point and accordance to the situation]." (33:70)

"O you who believe, fulfill the obligations." (5:1)

"Indeed Allah commands you to render back the trusts to whom they are due and when you judge then judge with justice" (4:58).

These verses do not differentiate between person and person or nation and nation or even Muslim and non-Muslim.

VI. THE STATE'S AFFAIRS SHOULD BE RESOLVED IN THE AGREEMENT WITH QURAN AND SUNNAH, THE RULES OF SHARIA.

Moreover, when there are no such instructions, then it may be resolved on the basis of *Shura* as we mentioned, even though the *Khalifa* is not bound to accept it as a whole. However, he should not throw it away as a whole either. It depends in brief we can say that its characteristics are:

i. THE SOVEREIGNTY OF ALLAH AND THE SUPREMACY OF THE QURAN AND SUNNAH

ii. OBEDIENCE TO ALLAH AND HIS MESSENGER

iii. FOLLOWING THE FOOTSTEPS OF THE MESSENGER OF ALLAH AND HIS *KHULAFA* (SUCCESSORS)

iv. THE CONCEPT OF *KHALAFAH*

v. THE *SHURA* (CONSULTATION) IS THE VISIBLE PRINCIPLE

vi. THE IMPLEMENTATION OF SHARIA TO PROVIDE A GOOD LIFE HERE IN THIS WORLD, THEY MAY ALL HAVE A GOOD ONE IN THE HEREAFTER

ADMINISTRATION

As we know, the *Khalifa* is the head of the state, the supreme commander of the forces, and the chief executive. So, he is the one responsible, but he needs people to help and support him to run state affairs smoothly. All these people are subject to the state, its laws, and rules. Also, to its policies from time to time, and all these come through or from the *Khalifa*, so they are subject to the *Khalifa*. The *Khalifa* or in his name can delegate the power to them in a particular field to a given limit. So, no one should step in an area other than his, nor should he cross the boundaries in the field concerned. Sharia puts and prescribes limits and bounds. Even the *Khalifa* will describe the same for others. Otherwise, they will create a mess and argue, and then nothing can be done correctly. The Prophet himself did this administrating, giving duties to others and delegating powers to the *Waalis* (governors and collectors). Then his successors Abu Bakr followed the same. Umar, the second successor, disciplined this in an organized way and so was the case of Uthman and Ali as well, and they are the predecessors of the *ummah*.

Allama Mawardi mentioned a few important departments:

I. Those who have the general power of attorney in all affairs, so they handle all these as agents of the *Khalifa*; in today's politics this might be equivalent to a prime minister.

II. The power of an inclusive authority but in specific affairs like the governors of different states.

III. Specific authority, like the chief justice in judicial affairs, chief of the army, auditor general, et cetera.

IV. Specific authority in distinct affairs like the judge in a particular jurisdiction power wise, or territorial, or the collector of a distinct area.

RESPONSIBILITIES OF THE PEOPLE APPOINTED BY THE KHALIFA

Allama Mawardi said these responsibilities are of two types:

A. *AL WAZARAH* OR MINISTRY

B. *AL IMARAH*

The first one is for those who were appointed by the *Khalifa* for the whole state. Moreover, there are two types,

a. *WAZEERUT TAFWEED*

Who has been given the authority to look into all the affairs of the state. Also, to resolve these to the best of his knowledge, planning, and ability and we can call it premiership in today's terminology. This appointee can do everything on behalf of the *Khalifa* except three things.

A. He cannot appoint someone for this post after him while the *Khalifa* can nominate a *Khalifa* after him, and he can also appoint another *Wazeerut Tafweed*.

B. The *Khalifa* can suspend the right to elect a *Khalifa*, but the *Wazeerut Tafweed* cannot do that.

C. The Khalifa can remove one who has been appointed by this *Wazir* (minister) but this *Wazir* cannot remove one who has been designated by the *Khalifa*.

If they both differed in an issue, then

(I) If that is in economic affairs, the *Khalifa* cannot nullify what the Wazir has done as long as that is not a big blunder.

(II) If the *Wazir* appointed someone as a *Wali* (governor) for example, and the *Khalifa* does not like him, then he can reject him.

(III) If they both appointed two different people to one post, then the first appointment is the one that is accepted.

To not have conflict, the *Wazir* must study the day-to-day business of the *Khalifa* so he may not do such a thing that contradicts something already done by the Imam. Also, the *Khalifa* may look into the daily business of the *Wazir* and approve what is right and to revoke what is not right, because these affairs were according to his deduction and approach, and it could be wrong. So, the *Khalifa* has the right to withdraw what is incorrect.

Then for such a *Wazir* all the required qualities of a *Khalifa* are required except the quality of being from Quraish, according to those who said that it is a must for the *Khalifa* to be from Quraish. Because Abu Bakr said to the *Ansar* we are *Ameer* and you are *Wazir*. Also, it is a must for *Wazir* to be from those who can deduce laws and to know the tax and army systems as well. It means that he has some knowledge of revenue collection, finance, and economics, and also on defense.

This responsibility may be given based on a contract between him and the *Khalifa*. In other words, the *Khalifa* has to take an oath from him; in this regard this *Wazir* must be only one individual just like the *Khalifa*.

Moreover, as for the *Wazeerut Taufeez* is concerned, he is a link between the Khalifa and the general public and the *Ameers* of different provinces or departments for example. He has two duties:

(I) To take the issues to the *Khalifa* which are important whatever they maybe.

(II) To take the orders of the *Khalifa* or his wishes to the people concerned.

It means that this *Wazir* cannot practice based on his personal deduction, approach, and planning, but only a sometimes when it is required urgently. This *Wazir* needs to be

(I) TRUSTWORTHY;

(II) TRUTHFUL;

(III) NOT AVARICIOUS;

(IV) UNBIASED TOWARDS THE PEOPLE CONCERNED;

(V) POSSESSED OF A STRONG MEMORY

(VI) CLEVER;

(VII) NOT TO BE FROM PEOPLE WHO FOLLOW THEIR WHIMS AND DESIRES

He also can be from amongst the non-Muslims (*Zimmi*) also, but could the *Wazir* be a woman? There are two views in this regard; that because of extra exposure needed for such a position that a woman may not be given this responsibility. Can the *Wazir* be more than one person? It depends on the circumstance.

Then *Wazeerut Tafweed* has much power, so he must be:

a. A FREE MAN (i.e., not a slave),

b. A MUSLIM,

c. POSSESSED OF TALENT TO DEDUCE LAWS,

d. KNOWLEDGEABLE ABOUT ECONOMICS AND DEFENSE, BUT THESE QUALITIES ARE NOT REQUIRED FOR THE *WAZEERUT TAUFEEZ*, TO BE A MAN IS MUST IN THE FIRST ONE BUT IN *WAZEERUT TAUFEEZ* THERE ARE TWO POINTS OF VIEWS.

e. THE FIRST ONE CAN DECIDE A MATTER HIMSELF BUT THE SECOND ONE CANNOT.

f. THE FIRST ONE CAN APPOINT A *WAALI* HIMSELF BUT THE SECOND ONE CANNOT.

g. *WAZEERUT TAFEED* CAN MAKE WAR AND PEACE PLANS BUT *WAZEERUT TAUFEEZ* CANNOT.

h. *WAZEERUT TAFWEED* CAN CARRY OUT THE REVENUE AND FINANCE AFFAIRS BUT THE *WAZEERUT TAUFEEZ* CANNOT

Nowadays we can call the first one as minister and the 2nd one as state minister

(II) AL-IMARAH

The second responsibility of the appointed people is *Al Imarah*. The appointment of *Ameers* in different areas was started in the time of Umar when the Islamic state was expanded to Sham, Persia, and Africa. He made Sham in two parts, Persia in three, and Africa in three as well. Each part had an appointed *Ameer* or *Waali* leading them in prayer, judging their disputes, collecting the revenue, and leading the army. The Umayyad adopted the same procedure, and Abbasids and later on the jurists classified this *Imarah* into two categories:

A. AL IMARATUL AAMMAH

This type includes all the affairs in the relevant zone like to maintain peace, defense, revenue, and the judicial procedure. This type is further classified into two subcategories:

1. IMARATUL-ISTIKFA

the *Khalifa* appoints someone well qualified in a particular zone. However, this is up to the Khalifa to hand him over all the affairs to specify the affairs he will be taking care of. Then that person has full authority over those affairs. If the *Khalifa* has appointed to a certain area and does not specify his fields of responsibility, then that *Imarah* is general and inclusive to all affairs of that zone. This *Ameer* has to take care of the following:

    I.   TO LOOK INTO THE ARMY AND ARMED FORCES AFFAIRS, THEIR PLANNING AND SALARIES, IF THE *KHALIFA* HAS NOT SEEN TO IT ALREADY

    II.   TO APPOINT JUDGES AND OFFICERS FOR THE SPECIFIED ZONE

III. TO COLLECT TAXES, TO APPOINT COLLECTORS AND TO ARRANGE HOW AND WHERE THE MONIES SHOULD BE SPENT

IV. THE PROTECTION OF *DEEN* AND ITS RULES.

V. TO UPHOLD BOTH LAWS AND RULES OF ALLAH AND THE RIGHTS OF HUMANITY

VI. TO LEAD THE FRIDAY AND EID PRAYERS EITHER HIMSELF, OR TO APPOINT SOMEONE TO DO SO ON HIS BEHALF

VII. TO EASE THE PERFORMANCE OF HAJJ (PILGRIMAGE TO MECCA)

Moreover, if that are is adjacent to another country to the ocean, then that *Ameer* is bound to safeguard the boundaries and to counter any attack from that place. The required qualities for such an Ameer are the qualities of *Wazeerut Tafweed*. The only difference is that the jurisdiction of this *Ameer* is in a particular zone while the jurisdiction of *Wazeerut Tafweed* is in the whole country. Also, this *Wazeerut Tafweed* has the right to look into the performance of zones. He can even depose an *Ameer* if he has appointed him. However, if the *Khalifa* has done it, then his deposition should be with the permission of the *Khalifa* or his later approval.

This *Ameer* or *Wali* can appoint *Wazeerut Taufeez* for his zone, and it can be one or more people, but he cannot appoint a *Wazeerut Tafweed* except with the permission of the *Khalifa*.

2. *IMARATUL ISTEELA*

Isteela means taking power and control by force. If someone gains power by force in a particular zone, then the Khalifa should approve him. Moreover, he should be allowed to manage the affairs of that zone, but the religious authority may remain with the *Khalifa*. This approval is because of necessity and the facts on the ground. Otherwise, he must be deposed. He may be deposed for the following reasons:

1. TO DEFEND THE *KHALAFAH* AND NOT TO GET INVOLVED IN A FIGHT WITH HIS PEOPLE AS IT TAKES AWAY THE RESPECT AND HONOR OF THE *KHALAFAH* AND DISTURBS THE SYSTEM.

2. TO KEEP THE RULE OF *DEEN* INTACT.

3. TO REMAIN UNITED.

4. TO HAVE THE RELIGIOUS AUTHORITIES AND THEIR DECREE AND JUDGMENTS ENFORCED AND IMPLEMENTED.

5. TO HAVE THE *ZAKAT* AND OTHER ECONOMIC RITUALS REVENUE DISTRIBUTED ACCORDING TO SHARIA.

6. TO IMPLEMENT RELIGIOUS PUNISHMENTS FOR CRIMES, INCLUDING EXECUTIONS.

7. TO ENSURE THAT THAT *AMEER* IS SUBMISSIVE TO ISLAM AND ITS RULES.

The difference between these two, i.e., *Imaratul Istikfa* and *Imaratul Isteela* is:

(I) *IMARATUL ISTIKFA* IS DONE BY THE SELECTION OF THE KHALIFA AND ACCEPTANCE OF THE *AMEER* CONCERNED, WHILE *IMARATUL ISTEELA* IS BY FORCE AND NECESSITY.

(II) *IMARATUL ISTIKFA* INCLUDES THE ZONE THE *KHALIFA* HAS MENTIONED IN THE CONTRACT, WHILE *IMARATUL ISTEELA* IS FOR THAT AREA IN WHICH HE HAS OBTAINED CONTROL BY FORCE.

(III) *IMARATUL ISTIKFA* INCLUDES THE AFFAIRS REFERRED TO BY THE *KHALIFA*, WHILE *IMARATUL ISTEELA* INCLUDES ALL THE AFFAIRS OF THE ZONE CONCERNED.

(IV) *IMARATUL ISTIKFA* CAN APPOINT A *WAZEERUT TAUFEEZ* BY HIMSELF, BUT *WAZEERUT TAFWEED* CAN ONLY APPOINT WITH THE PERMISSION OF THE *KHALIFA*. *IMARATUL ISTEELA* CAN APPOINT BOTH TYPES HIMSELF.

B. *AL IMARATUL KHASSAH*

Originally in Islam the concept of *Imarat* was general and included all the affairs like executive, judiciary, defense, revenue, et cetera. That was the case of Amr Ibn Aas, who conquered Misr (Egypt). Also, he was the governor, the collector, the judge, and the general as well. Then Umar appointed Abdullah Ibn Abi Sarah as the collector, Kab Ibn Soor as the judge, and the governor remained the Imam and the general.

This gave us the concept of three branches of government. The legislative branch is the duty of the jurists. The enforcement of law and to maintain order and peace is the responsibility of the executive branch. The judicial procedure is the jurisdiction of the judiciary system. The army is an entirely separate entity, of which the *Khalifa* is the commander.

All these details are given from the Islamic state's history on how they used to manage these affairs. However, nowadays there are written constitutions, rules, laws, and policies. Areas of jurisdiction, provinces, counties, federation, unions, federating units, and states in the union are clearly mentioned. Also mentioned are the administration for the center and the states or provinces, their various departments, its heads, officers, and workers their jurisdiction and duties. Finally, the common things controlled by the center and the powers of the different zones, states, and provinces in a country, everything, is mentioned. All the people, especially those in authority, are bound to follow the rules of these institutions. If the people in power do not follow that, then the higher authority should act in this regard, or even the public can go against them to the judiciary court. People have adopted these various concepts from time to time, and whenever they feel that such and such thing is not practical anymore, they either replace it or modify it. So, as we said Islam has given principles and left a vast field for intellect. Intellectuals should think, deduce, and implement what is best for the state and public to meet the needs of the time, provided it is not against the supreme and fundamental law of Islam, i.e., the Holy Quran and the Sunnah.

JUDICIARY

As we mentioned before, many governments are divided into three branches. One important branch is the legislative branch. In Islam, it is the duty of the jurists to deduce and frame the laws for issues, especially those that do not have any expressed or deduced solution from the Quran or the Sunnah. As the Prophet asked Muaaz Ibn Jabal when he was sending him as an *Ameer* and *Qazi* (judge) to Yemen, "how will you judge?" Muaaz said, "I will judge based on the Quran." The Prophet then asked, "and if you could not find it [there]? Muaaz said, "In that case, I would rule based on the Sunnah of the Prophet." The Prophet said and if you could not find it [there either]? He said, "then I would deduce [and apply] my [juristic] opinion [analogical deduction]. The Prophet said, "praise be to Allah, who empowered the messenger of his messenger towards what he likes."

Issues and disputes will arise, so authority and judgment are needed. This is reasonable and logical. One of the main purposes of "Deen" is to provide peace and justice, and that is to be rendered by an authority that has control. For judgment, the judge and a judiciary system are needed. Justice is the order of Allah and being just is Allah's attribute. To be a judge and to administer the justice based on Quran and Sunnah, Ibn Masud said that,

> "If someone will do that between two parties is more pleasing to me than worship for seventy years."

The Prophet of Allah was the head of the state, the chief executive, the supreme commander, the legislator, and the judge. His noble personality gathered the executive, legislative, and judiciary branches together. Yes, he sent Ali and Muaaz Ibn Jabal to Yemen as judges, and when he conquered Makah, then he appointed Atab Ibn Aseed as *Ameer* and judge in Makah.

Umar was a judge in the time of Abu Bakr. In the time of Umar, as we said, he separated the judiciary from executive to some extent and appointed judges in different parts of the country. Umar wrote a letter to Abu Musa, which is considered a rule and regulation for the judiciary, judicial procedure, and judges. He also established different departments and also prisons. The judges used to deal with civil suits, financial, and property disputes, while the criminal side, i.e., *Qisas* and *Hudood* were the jurisdiction of the *Khalifa* and the *Waalis* of the states. However, Uthman established a specific judiciary and judicial premises.

THE JUDICIARY WAS BASED UPON TWO THINGS:

(I) THE JUDGE

(II) NO COMPILATION OF THE DECREES OF THE JUDGE AS IT WAS TO BE EXECUTED AT THE SAME TIME UNDER THE SUPERVISION OF THE *QAZI* (JUDGE).

Umar also fixed salaries for these judges so they may have free time (i.e., not need to work more to supplement their income) and a clear mind to think only about their job and duty.

In their decree, they used to go to the Quran, Sunnah, Ijma, and Qiyas. The Umayyad and Abbasids adopted the same procedure in the proceeding times, so the judges were free to their jobs, duties, and power. Also, the Umayyads started recording the procedure, and there were distinct types of judges based on skill and specialties. The Abbasids introduced the post of a chief justice, and the first chief justice was Qazi Abu Yusuf, the student of Imam Abu Hanifa. His status was similar to that of the justice minister, who used to appoint the judges and oversaw them as well. Also, the black robe or gown for judges was introduced at that time of Khalifa Harun Rashid for Qazi Abu Yusuf.

THE QUALITIES OF THE JUDGES

The Khalifa is the center of power and authority, so naturally he has the right to appoint judges, or the *Wazeerut Tafweed* can do that, as we mentioned. The *Ameer* of a particular state can also appoint judges in his region.

THE JUDGES MUST HAVE THE FOLLOWING QUALITIES

(I) TO BE A MUSLIM;

(II) TO BE AN ADULT;

(III) TO BE OF SOUND MIND;

(IV) TO HAVE FULL COMMAND OF HIS FACULTIES, SO HE MAY NOT BE BLIND, DEAF, OR MUTE.

(V) TO HAVE AUTHENTIC, DETAILED KNOWLEDGE OF SHARIA.

These are qualities required in a judge in all four schools of jurisprudence while there are some other requirements like;

(I) TO BE ADL AND JUST

This is a condition according to three schools of jurisprudence. So, a *Fasiq*, one who has sinned or one whose testimony is rejected because of false charges he put against someone may not be appointed as a judge, because he is not trustworthy.

Allah said:

> *"O you who believe! If a* Fasiq *brought you the news, then inquire[about] it." - (49:6)*

So, one whose testimony is not accepted may not be appointed as a judge. However, the Hanafis say that although it is not good if a *Fasiq* is appointed to the post, if it is done then that is all right. It is like his testimony that the judge should not accept it. If he did and judged an issue based on that, then his verdict is legal. Moreover, it is a sin on the part of the judge. However, one who is charged with *Qazaf* and false charges may not be given the post, nor may his testimony be accepted according to the Hanafis.

(II) THE JUDGE HAS TO BE A MAN

This is a condition of three schools of jurisprudence. So, a woman may not be appointed as a magistrate because judges have a type of *Walayat* (authority like a *Khalifa*). As women cannot be *Khalifa*, so they cannot be a judge as well. However, the Hanafis say, because women can be a witness in social and civil cases, she can be a judge as well. However, in *Qisas* and *Hudood* she cannot testify so she cannot be a judge in that field, as

(I) Allah has mentioned her testimony in civil cases and said,

> *"And get two witnesses out of your own men, and if there are no two men [available] then [get] one man*

and two women from those whom you like as witnesses, so that if one of them errs [forgets] then the other one will remind her" - (2:282)

Ibn Rushd relates from Ibn Jarir At-Tabari that according to him, women can be judges in both civil and criminal cases because they can give Fatwa in either field. To us what the Hanafis say seems to be more just because human nature is that they do not forgive and forget the person that is a witness against them, especially in criminal procedure. So, to protect women from the aftereffects of that, Allah has dropped them from that side of testimony as a mercy and protection. It is the same case with *Qada*. Also, women have a very soft nature and show mercy more frequently than men. In a criminal procedure that is not a good tendency to have.

(III) THE TALENT AND CAPABILITY OF IJTIHAD ARE OTHER REQUIREMENTS OF A QADI ACCORDING TO THREE SCHOOLS OF JURISPRUDENCE AND SOME HANAFIS ALSO

So, a *Muqallid*, even though he is an *Aalim* (scholar), may not be appointed as a judge because the judgment may be on the basis of Quran and Sunnah. However, the *madhab* of the Hanafis is that to be a *Mujtahid* is recommended but that is not a requirement, so an *Aalim*, who is qualified in *Fiqh* and Sharia, is eligible for this job. Especially when the entire body of *Fiqh* is compiled and clarified, it is fine for a *Muqallid* to be a judge. Moreover, in today's world a *Mujtahid Mutlaq* is not found anywhere. That is why the later scholars of the other three schools of jurisprudence echoed what the Hanafis said. The only thing is that an overqualified scholar who is known for his character, honesty, and piety may be given priority.

The judge is bound to look into the rules of Sharia regarding the issue, and he must implement that. Moreover, as we said, *Fiqh* is confidential nowadays, so there is no difficulty for a qualified jurist. The only thing for him is only to look into the specific rule whether that applies to this case and issue or not, and if that is, then he may apply that without any reservation or hesitation.

There can be a problem where the opinion of his Imam cannot be implemented appropriately in the particular circumstances, they are in. So, then he may look for the view of any other authentic jurist of the same *Fiqh* or even for the opinion of another recognized *Fiqh* (Madhab). The duty of a judge is to dispense justice and safeguard rights. If there is no solution for that issue, then if he has the ability, he may deduce a solution for the issue following the established procedures and rules for that. Alternatively, he may ask another capable jurist for his opinion.

For the procedure and judgment, he must be committed to the evidence, proof, testimony, documents, admission, customs, denial, and oath, et cetera.

All jurists have said that the judge must avoid blame from any side and any type. The judge may not judge in a case in which he has any personal interest therein or any enmity for the individuals that are involved. Also, he may not hear a case of brought by a close relation such as a parent, child or grandchild, or spouse.

There are certainly other things as well, which should be taken into consideration:

1. HE SHOULD CONSULT OTHER QUALIFIED JURISTS IF THE CASE IS VERY COMPLICATED.

2. HE SHOULD NOT BE BIASED TOWARDS ONE PARTY IN ANY WAY.

3. HE SHOULD NOT ACCEPT GIFTS ESPECIALLY, FROM THE PARTIES INVOLVED, AS THIS IS CONSIDERED A BRIBE.

4. HE SHOULD NOT ACCEPT INVITATIONS FROM THOSE WHO WERE HIS FRIENDS BEFORE AND ESPECIALLY THE INVITATION TO EITHER SIDE OF THE CASE.

The judiciary is bound to make the procedure accessible and to provide facilities to those who come to them. Also, if at any time the *Qazi* feels any tension, then he should not hear the case.

He may try to convince the parties to reconcile if the case is compoundable. Also, he may try his best to find out what type of person the witness to the case is, because *Tazkiyatush-Shuhud* is important for proper procedure.

The state may provide beneficial sources and facilities to the judge so they may not think of corruption and to give them and their decrees proper respect, protection, and to execute their decrees.

Also, their job may not be interrupted, nor they may be deposed for no reason or petty things even though the appointing authority has the authority to depose him.

THE TYPES OF JUDGES

Allama Al Mawardi said that judges are of four types:

1. A judge in general: he can judge any issue relating to anyone, anywhere in the country, and anytime. This includes ten things:

(I) To judge disputes and conflicts as a settlement or as a trial and judgment.

(II) To take the rights of someone when that is proven in the court with due process.

(III) Guardianship of one who does not have the capability of a normal adult, such as an insane person or a minor. Also, one who lost his wealth because of being extravagant or insolvency to put bans on their transactions for example. However, this second type is according to the three schools and also according to Abu Yusuf and Muhammad.

Abu Hanifa said,

"No ban or restrictions may be put on a person's financial actions and transactions as long as s/he is an *adult and sane. Because that goes against basic dignity and freedom. Yes, if those people whom someone owes went to court and in order to get their money returned then after due process, the court will order him to sell his belongings and to pay them."*

(IV) To look into endowments, to protect them and to save and spend them appropriately.

(V) To execute wills and testaments faithfully.

(VI) To marry widows to the suitable men if they do not have guardians; this is the view of three Imams, while according to Abu Hanifa an adult woman cannot be forced into *Nikah*.

(VII) To carry out the *Hudood* (fixed punishment in Quran and Sunnah) but if that is the right of Allah, then the judge himself is responsible for that. However, if that is the right of a human then after his complaint, he may do that.

(VIII) To look into the benefit of the general public so if there is anything which is harmful to the public in the streets, roads, or bazaars, he may stop it. However, the view of Abu Hanifa is that he should only look into it if someone brings it to his attention; he should not take preemptive action himself.

(IX) To keep oneself up to date about his subordinate judges and to select his subordinates as well.

(X) To deal with everyone with equanimity whether rich or poor, powerful, or weak, and not to follow his own desires in any way,

As Allah said:

"O you who believe! Stand out firmly for justice as witness to Allah, even though it be against yourselves or your parents or your kin if he [the party to a case] in rich or poor, Allah is superior to them both so follow not the desire so you may do justice; and whether you remain distant or not, Allah is all acquainted with what you do." - (4:135)

This verse made it clear that judges must follow the law and legal procedure and not be biased, either to a wealthy individual because of his wealth nor to a poor person out of sympathy. Because you represent Allah, and you are subject to him so follow what He and His laws say. Otherwise, you do not follow *Deen* but your desires. For either you will turn your face from the laws of Allah, or you will distort it, and that is a form of cheating to Allah and yourself.

2. A judge in a particular field and jurisdiction. So, he may confine himself to his jurisdiction and field (like the judge of a county, district, or as state, or the judge for the cases of income tax or custom, et cetera).

3. A judge whose jurisdiction is limited to an area even though he is looking into all the things above we mentioned.

4. A judge for a particular day, for example, Friday, so he will look into these matters and judge only on Friday.

THE APPOINTMENT OF JUDGES

The authority in general is with the *Khalifa*; he has the power to appoint a judge. However, if he has delegated the powers to someone else like *Wazeerut Tafweed* or the *Ameer* in a particular state, then they also can appoint the judges.

THERE ARE FOUR REQUIRED CONDITIONS:

(I) THE ONE WHO APPOINTS THE JUDGE MUST HAVE THIS AUTHORITY AND THE JUDGE MUST KNOW THAT.

(II) THE REQUIRED QUALITIES OF A MAGISTRATE ARE FOUND IN THE APPOINTEE, AND THE APPOINTING AUTHORITY KNOWS ABOUT THEM.

(III) THE POWER JURISDICTION AND FIELD OF HIS JOB AS MENTIONED.

(IV) THE TERRITORIAL JURISDICTION, ALSO AS MENTIONED.

The appointing authority can depose a judge, but he should not do that without very good reason. If he has been deposed, then this may be conveyed to him. The view of the Hanafis is that this deposition is not a one-sided case. So, after his deposition but before being informed, all his decrees are legal and may be executed. He can also resign, but he should not do that unless he has a reasonable excuse, as this is the best type of worship because it is for the benefit of the general public.

He is not replaced in the event of the death of the appointing authority, because he does not work for the Khalifa in person but as a representative of the general public and they are there. It is the same case if the appointing authority is deposed.

The Hanafis, some Shafis, and some Hanbalis said that the hearing of a case by a group of judges is also allowed. If they cannot agree on the decision, then the majority's decision may be taken.

The basic concept is that there should be one verdict. However, the fear of injustice is there in these later times, due to people not having exemplary piety and fear of Allah. That is why Islam did not forbid accepting the verdict of a lower judge to a higher one, even though there might be legal access to the same upper judge for review or revision. In this regard we can present two stories. One is that of Ali, when he judged between two people and told them that if they were not happy with his ruling then they could take it to the Prophet of Allah. They did so, and the Prophet approved the decree of Ali. Also, Umar wrote his famous letter to Abu Musa al Ash'ari, which can be considered a fundamental document for judiciary and judges. He informed him that when you passed a verdict in a case and later on you changed your mind, then the original verdict should not prevent a judge from changing his ruling to follow the right concept he found later on.

However, here we will say that if the decree is based on a text of the Quran or Sunnah or Ijma then the altered concept is wrong. If that first decree is against the Quran and Sunnah, then it is void and must be nullified. However, if that decree was based on his opinion and deduction, and then his deduction and opinion changed, then as both are based upon deduction so the first decree may not be altered. However, for a similar case the decision may be according to the new deduction. As Umar said in such an issue, that the first was as we decreed then, and this later one is as we decreed now. However, now when there are upper-level courts or appellate courts, one can take any decision of the lower court to the upper one, and they will investigate it. However, when that ultimate court delivers a verdict in a case, then it is final even though their opinion might change later, because deduction could not be nullified by the like of that, as the first deduction already has judicial support. However, that cannot be precedence in the future if the opinion of the same judge was changed later.

A judge's verdict cannot make a lawful thing unlawful or vice versa. Also, it does not produce rights; rather, it clarifies if there is any ambiguity therein.

As the Prophet of Allah said,

> *"After a decree that may be one of you is more soft spoken and proved his case. If I have decreed with something in his favor from the rights of his brother, he should not take it, because I cut for him nothing but a piece of the fire."*

However, Imam Abu Hanifa said that the decree of a judge is executed in contracts and annulments of contracts. So, if someone claimed that a woman was his wife, and he proved it in the court and the judge decreed it, accordingly, based on this decree she would become his wife even if in reality, there was no *Nikah* and no marriage ceremony performed. It is the same with the case of divorce: if the wife proves it, and the judge decrees it, then the couple are divorced.

THESE TYPES OF CASES HAVE TWO CONDITIONS:

(I) THE JUDGE DOES NOT KNOW FOR SURE THAT THE WITNESSES ARE LYING.

(II) THE ISSUE CONCERNED MAY BE OF A NATURE THAT HE WAS AUTHORIZED TO PERFORM HIMSELF AT THE TIME OF THIS DECREE, LIKE *NIKAH* OR DIVORCE.

TAHKEEM (ARBITRATION)

When two parties agree upon someone to judge between him and her, this is called *Tahkeem*. This is a legal concept in Islam. Allah said regarding disputes between husband and wife:

> *"And if you fear a breach between them, then appoint an arbitrator from her family and another one from his family, if they both intend a peace [reconciliation] Allah will make a patch up between them."* - *(4:35)*

The Prophet himself agreed to the arbitration of Sad Ibn Muaaz with the Jews of Bani Quraizah when they cheated the state and the Prophet accepted and executed his decision.

The arbitrator should have the qualities of a *Qazi* (judge) but as we said that if a *Fasiq* is appointed as a judge, then that is acceptable according to the Hanafis. It is the same if a non-scholar is appointed because he can ask and consult another scholar. The arbitration could be only in financial and family matters. There is no arbitration in *Hudood* and *Qisas* even in the case of *Qatli - Khata* (manslaughter. Reconciliation can take place either for free or for something less than the blood money (restitution).

There can be more than one arbitrator like there can be more than one judge. The verse we quoted before has mentioned two, one from the husband's side and one from the wife's side.

If the arbitrator has not given his verdict, either party can withdraw its consent, because it was based on mutual consent, and that may remain until the verdict. However, Imam Malik said that as they started it with mutual consent, so the withdrawal should be done in the same way.

When the arbitrator gives his decision, then that they are ethically and socially bound to follow it. If that is taken to a court later so if that is following the law, then the judge should endorse the ruling of the arbitrator because there is no benefit to undoing it.

WILAYATUL MAZALIM

This is the case of the *Khalifa*, the *Wazeerut Tafweed*, *Wazeerut Tafweez*, and the *Ameers* of different areas: to investigate the wrong-doings of people in authority or in power where the common judicial system does not act. This is the responsibility of the Khalifa, and then the people mentioned above, but the *Khalifa* or *Wazeerut Tafweed* or the *Ameer* of a state can appoint a particular person or persons for the said purpose. This person or persons must have the qualities of a *Khalifa*, a *Wazeerut Tafweed*, or an *Ameer*, which is almost the same. The Prophet of Allah himself used to investigate the *Mazalim* as he sent Ali to pay the blood money to the people killed by Khalid as a mistake, from the tribe of Bani Juzaimah. Umar was strict regarding *Mazalim*. He stuck up for a Coptic man when he was insulted by Governor Amr Ibnul Aas. Ali also investigated it when his taking charge of Khalifa was delayed for a few days and some *Mazalim* happened there.

Abdul Malik from the Umayyad Dynasty set aside a specific day to hear these cases. Umar Ibn Abdul Aziz returned property to the people had been wrongfully seized by his predecessors. The Abbasid *Khalifas*, like Al Mahdi, Al Hadi, Al Rashid, Al Mamoon, and Al Muhtadi, also adopted this procedure. They gave the rights back to the people.

For the purpose as mentioned earlier, even a department could be established, consisting of judges, officers, police, and jurists. The duties of such a person or persons are:

To look into the performance of those in authority whether they follow Sharia or not. Moreover, whether they have done any wrong to the public in general or to individuals physically or financially. Also, to look into the records of the different department if needed. For the purpose mentioned above, they can act because this is either a matter of the interest of the general public or a violation of fundamental rights.

To investigate the salaries of those in services, to determine whether it is reasonable or not and whether they receive it at the same time or is it delayed. If the authorities have usurped the property of someone or people in authority, then he/they can act. For such an action, the complaint of the usurped one is not required. He/they can do that whether they have taken it for their selves or the state and government. He/they do not need the owner to bring forward proof; the estate's documents are enough. However, if individuals who are powerful and the case have usurped that is brought to them, then they must look into it properly if they filed an application with them. Then they can decide the case accordingly either based on the confession of the usurper or on their personal knowledge that this wrong has been done to the applicant or based on the testimony, or that the general public say it, and there is no doubt in it.

Also, their responsibility is to investigate the *Auqaf* for public affairs whether the production or benefits of that endowment is spent in its aforementioned ways or not. He can find it with the record and documents, or other sources and support. In case of endowment for some specific individuals or a particular group, he can look into it if the complaint by such persons. Alternatively, a group came to him but in the first one any claim is not a must. Instead, they can take a *suo moto* action.

Another duty of theirs is to execute the decrees of other courts that could not normally be executed because the person/persons are powerful against whom the decree is issued. Also, they may look into those things the *Hisbah* or ombudsmen cannot investigate. Their other responsibility is to look into open types of worship like Friday prayer, Eid prayer, Hajj, and Jihad if they are not done properly. They may investigate the performance of the judges and the way they heard a case, and whether they followed the due process or not. However, they can only do this if a party or parties brought a similar complaint to them.

THE DIFFERENCES BETWEEN THE JUDGES AND *WALI UL MAZALIM*:

ALLAMA MAWARDI MENTIONED A FEW DIFFERENCES:

1. THE JUDGES CANNOT USE HARD LANGUAGE ABOUT EITHER PARTY, BUT *WALI UL MAZALIM* CAN DO SO.

2. THE JUDGE'S FIELD IS LIMITED ALONG WITH HIS WORDS, BUT THE *WALI UL MAZALIM* HAS A VAST ONE.

3. *WALI UL MAZALIM* CAN USE OTHER SOURCES AND MEANS OF PROVING OTHER THAN THE METHODS APPROVED FOR A JUDGE.

4. THE *WALI UL MAZALIM* CAN DISCIPLINE A WRONGDOER, BUT A JUDGE CANNOT DO SO.

5. THE *WALI UL MAZALIM* CAN DELAY WHEN HE FEELS SOME AMBIGUITY WHILE JUDGES HAVE TO DECIDE THE CASE WHEN THE PARTY OR PARTIES REQUEST IT.

6. THE *WALI UL MAZALIM* CAN PUSH THE PARTIES TOWARDS RECONCILIATION, BUT A JUDGE CANNOT UNLESS THE PARTIES ASK FOR IT.

7. THE *WALI UL MAZALIM* CAN LIMIT THE PARTY'S MOVEMENT SO THEY MAY AGREE TO MUTUAL JUSTICE BETWEEN THEM.

8. THE JUDGES CAN ONLY TAKE THE TESTIMONY OF AN *ADL* AND JUST WITNESS. THE *WALI UL MAZALIM* CAN ACCEPT THE DEPOSITION OF ONE WHOSE STATUS HE DOES NOT KNOW.

9. IF HE WANTS, THE *WALI UL MAZALIM* CAN ASK THE WITNESS TO GIVE HIS STATEMENT UNDER OATH BUT THITAT IS NOT FOR A NORMAL AUTHORITY TO REQUEST FOR AN OATH.

10. THE JUDGES CAN COMPEL THE PLAINTIFFS TO BRING FORTH WITNESSES IF THERE ARE ANY WHILE THE *WALI UL MAZALIM* CAN ASK FOR WITNESSES HIMSELF TO HEAR FROM THEM IF THEY HAVE ANY INFORMATION ABOUT THE PROPERTIES.

These are the fundamental and golden ideas given by the jurists and scholars. However, in today's world all these concepts and ideas are in written and codified form approved by the authority. So, there are lower courts, superior courts, high courts, and the Supreme Court. Also, there are appellate courts as well.

The important thing is that the *Wali Ul Mazalim* has the judicial and executive powers both. The common people submit to courts and the decrees. However, the people in authority and the influential people very rarely submit to it, so they need a court with the special power of execution as well.

AL HISBAH (OMBUDSMAN)

This word is from the three root letters *Ha*, *Seen*, and *Baa*, and in the Arabic language Hasiba means "he thought," or "he counted." However, another word that can be derived from those same radical letters is *Ihtisab*, which means "accountability." So *Hisbah* means putting to accountability, but as a term in Sharia it means to enjoin good when it is deserted in totality and to prevent vice when that is done openly. The purpose of *Hisbah* is to protect and defend the society. Moreover, to help it, it is related to the social system, norms, values, and sometimes in harms and injuries, which need an immediate decision. As we know that to enjoin good and to prevent vice is the duty of the government and the general public as well. Allah said:

> *"Those who if we give them power in the land, they order for prayer, and to pay* Zakat, *they enjoin good and prevent vice and with Allah is the end of [all] matters." - (22:41)*

> *"You are the best* Ummah *raised up for mankind to enjoin good and to prevent vice and to believe in Allah." - (3:110)*

Imam Tirmizi narrated that the Prophet was passing by many bags of wheat in a bazaar. When he put his hand in a bag, he found wet wheat covered by dry wheat and he said, "Whoever deceived us, he is not from us." This is the proof that the Prophet did *Hisbah*, but Umar adopted this as a system and department, and this name *Hisbah* was introduced in the time of Al Mahdi from the Abbasid Dynasty.

As we said, it is the duty of every Muslim to promote virtue and to forbid and prevent vice and evil. Allah said:

> *"Why do not the Rabbis and the learned scholars forbid them from uttering sinful words and from eating illegal things? How bad is what they used to perform."* - (5:63)

> *"They used not to forbid one another from the* Munkar *[wrong deeds] which they did Vile indeed was what they used to do."* - (5:79)

Also, the Prophet said,

> *"Whoever from amongst you saw an evil he may change it with his hands, if he could not then with his tongue and if he couldn't then with his heart and that is the weakest Iman." (Muslim)*

However, for someone enjoining good and forbidding evil by himself, this is a matter of reward, and he is called *Mutatawwi*. Someone appointed for the purpose of enjoining good and forbidding vice is called *Al Muhtasib*.

ALLAMA MAWARDI MENTIONED SOME DIFFERENCES BETWEEN THE TWO:

a) THIS IS A PERSONAL RESPONSIBILITY OF THE *MUHTASIB*, AS HE IS APPOINTED FOR THAT JOB SO HE MUST DO THAT. HOWEVER, IT IS ALSO A COLLECTIVE RESPONSIBILITY OF THE UMMAH. SO, IF ONE FROM THE COMMUNITY DOES IT, HE GETS

THE REWARD, AND THE REST OF THE COMMUNITY ARE FREE FROM THAT RESPONSIBILITY.

b) A *MUHTASIB* MUST RESPOND POSITIVELY IF HE IS CALLED FOR DUTY, BUT THAT IS NOT THE CASE WITH OTHERS.

c) THE *MUHTASIB* MUST INVESTIGATE IF ANY WRONG IS GOING ON, OR ANY GOOD IS DESERTED IN TOTALITY. THEN HE MUST CARRY ON HIS DUTY IN THIS REGARD, BUT A *MUTATAWWI* IS NOT BOUND TO INVESTIGATE. HOWEVER, IF HE FOUND SUCH A THING, THEN HE MAY GO AHEAD AND STOP IT IF IT IS WRONG.

d) THE *MUHTASIB* CAN TAKE SOME SUBORDINATES WITH HIM, BUT THE *MUTATAWWI* CANNOT, AS THIS WILL BE COUNTERPRODUCTIVE.

e) THE *MUHTASIB* CAN USE HIS INTELLECT IN CUSTOMS LIKE SALE AND PURCHASE IN THE BAZAARS OR ENCROACHMENTS, FOR EXAMPLE, BUT OTHERS CANNOT DO SO.

The qualities of a *Muhtasib* are to be just, to have an opinion, be strong in matters of *Deen* and be aware of different types of vices. However, to be from those who can deduce is not required according to the majority of jurists. Some others have said that it is a must for him to be able to deduce. Their reasoning is that the judge can consult others and ask for their advice, but in certain cases the *Muhtasib* must decide immediately, so he needs to be a judge.

The characteristics of *Muhtasib* are that his responsibility has the shape of the judiciary, *Mazalim*, police and executive at the same time. So, he looks into the issues of consumer fraud and the cheating in scales and weighing. In this regard, he is like a judge. Also, he will give a chastisement to one who is openly committing sins. Alternatively, if he is doing things against the etiquettes of Islam, then in this regard he is like *Wali Ul Mazalim*. He will also investigate the general system of the society and its discipline and the peace in streets and bazaars. So, in this circumstance he is just like the police and public safety department. Allama Mawardi said his duty is to enjoin good and forbid evil, and this is related to:

a) THE RIGHTS OF ALLAH, WHICH INCLUDES *IBAADAAT* (WORSHIP) AND THE RIGHTS OF THE SOCIETY AND GENERAL PUBLIC.

b) THE OWNERSHIP RIGHTS OF INDIVIDUALS.

c) RIGHTS THAT ARE COMMON TO ALLAH AND THE INDIVIDUAL, BUT IN THIS REGARD THE WELFARE OF THE SOCIETY OR THE INDIVIDUAL ARE GIVEN PRIORITY.

REGARDING *AL AMR BIL MARUF* OR TO ENJOIN IN GOOD,

(A) It will be either related to the rights of Allah alone but will be relating to groups or and considered as symbols of *Deen* like *Aazaan* for prayer or not praying Friday prayer in the masjid.

Alternatively, even if that is not a symbol that is a must like prayer and fasting. That will be related to individuals so he may show attitude to the person if one is delaying prayer from its own time without any just cause.

(B) It will be related to the rights of people and that will either be:

(I) General: if the public needs and interests are being suspended; for example, drinking water or the masjid is being damaged. So, he may order for its repair either from the public exchequer, or he will ask the rich to do it.

(II) Alternatively, it can be specific rights like if someone is not paying back those who lent him money. Or not fulfilling his duties to those he is responsible for, like food and shelter for his children, parents, or wife. However, for this the deserving one may ask for it.

(III) Alternatively, the common rights of Allah and the people, so he will order divorces or separated women to fulfill their *Iddat*. If they do not then, he may give them chastisement, but not to the guardians if they do not marry their daughters, sisters, or nieces for example. Also, he may order the people to feed their cattle properly and not overburden them.

Regarding forbidding of evils, it will either be

(I) Relating to the rights of Allah and these are of three types:

i. Worship - He will give chastisement to one who does not take care of their prayer, or they do not fast without any just cause. Also, he will take *Zakat*, and if someone is begging as a profession, he may prevent it. If some unqualified person is giving *Fatwa* or spreading un-Islamic things in the society, he will stop him.

ii. Prohibited Things - He may stop people from places that create some doubts like the mingling of men and women in public. However, if the prohibited things are not out in the open, he may not spy on them, as Allah said, "and do not do any spying."

iii. Prohibited Transactions - He may also give a chastisement for usury or voidable contracts like cheating, fraud, or selling counterfeit goods.

(II) In the rights of humans, like harming the neighbors by exceeding the limits of one's property, such as when the branches of one's trees are causing trouble for the neighbors. However, in these cases a complaint is a must.

(III) Related to common rights like stopping people from standing upon the houses of others and to halt the Imam from lengthy prayers that weaken the old, sick, and disabled. Also, to stop people from overloading their buses, trucks, carriages. Another thing is stopping them from driving in dangerous weather or situations. Also, he will check the streets, bazaars, and public places if someone is creating any obstructions.

THE COMPARISON BETWEEN JUDICIARY, *WILAYTUL MAZALIM* AND HISBAH

All three of these are a type of the judiciary system in its general sense, but *Wilaytul Mazalim* is at the top level; following that is the judiciary, and then the *Hisbah*.

THE RESEMBLANCE BETWEEN JUDICIARY AND HISBAH

Allama Mawardi said:

(I) The complaint could be taken to both a judge and a *Muhtasib* regarding cheating on weights and measurement, or cheating in goods and money and its quality, or regarding delays in payments of loans and giving of rights. A *Muhtasib's* confinement to these three types is because his jurisdiction to help people to get their rights.

(II) In cases where he has the right of hearing, he is just like a judge so he can make a defendant to pay what he thinks is appropriate, but

a) The *Muhtasib* (ombudsman) cannot hear the cases of other than the wrongs above, as that is the jurisdiction of the judges.

b) He can hear those rights and order where the defendant admitted, and if he denied the claim, then that is the case of the judges.

c) The *Muhtasib* can take an action in his jurisdiction without a complainant and plaintiff, but a judge cannot, as a dispute between two people is concerned.

d) The *Muhtasib* should be stern in dealing and showing authority, but a judge should have both compassion and seriousness.

So, in the first two the position of a *Muhtasib* is lower than a judge but in the last two he is higher than the judge.

THE COMPARISON BETWEEN *HISBAH* AND *WILAYATUL MAZALIM*

The similarities are:

(I) Both should have strictness in dealings and showing authority.

(II) In their jurisdiction, they both can take an action without a complainant.

While they differ in:

(I) *Hisbah* is for those issues that do not need to be taken to the judges, while *Wilaytul Mazalim* is in issues that the judiciary system cannot tackle.

(II) The *Wali Ul Mazalim* can order things but the *Muhtasib* cannot.

However, in today's world different countries have different systems, so sometimes the judiciary system has the power of Wilayah, and they investigate those issues that could not be dealt with easily.

INTERNATIONAL RELATIONS

Islam is *Deen* and a complete system for everyone, every time, and every place. It qualifies the needs as Allah said:

> *"This day I perfected for you, your* **Deen** *and completed upon you, my favor and chosen for you Islam as* **Deen** *[system]." - (5:3)*

Also, He said:

> *"Enter into Islam in totality." - (2:208)*

THIS DEEN, AS WE HAVE SAID IS:

(a) THE *DEEN* OF ALLAH.

(b) THE *DEEN* OF ALL THE PROPHETS.

(c) THE *DEEN* OF HUMANS IN GENERAL.

THIS DEEN HAS FOUR BRANCHES:

(I) FAITH AND BELIEF.

(II) ETHICS AND CHARACTER.

(III) DEEDS AND ACTION.

(IV) DUTIES AND RESPONSIBILITIES.

1. THE PILLARS OF FAITH ARE KNOWN, AND THAT IS:

   i. BELIEF IN ALLAH.

   ii. BELIEF IN HIS ANGELS.

   iii. BELIEF IN HIS BOOKS.

   iv. BELIEF IN HIS PROPHETS.

   v. BELIEF IN THE DAY OF JUDGEMENT

   vi. BELIEF IN PRE-ORDAINED DIVINE LAW.

   vii. BELIEF IN LIFE AFTER DEATH.

2. CHARACTER IS:

   i. JUSTICE FOR ALL (SOCIAL JUSTICE).

   ii. KINDNESS TO THE WORLD AND ITS CREATURES.

   iii. FORGIVENESS IF SOMEONE HAS DONE WRONG TO YOU AS A MISTAKE, AND HE IS ASHAMED OF WHAT HE HAS DONE.

iv. Not to get into arguments with a stubborn, hard-headed person.

3. DEEDS ARE OF TWO TYPES:

(I) THOSE RELATED TO ALLAH, WHICH ARE *IBAADAAT* AND MANDATORY WORSHIP. ALSO, THE FIVE PILLARS OF ISLAM: PRAYER, FASTING, *ZAKAT*, HAJJ AND, OF COURSE, THE *KALIMAH* OR DECLARATION OF ISLAM.

(II) IN RELATION TO FELLOW HUMANS, AND THESE ARE:

(III) MARRIAGE AND ALL ITS ATTACHMENTS.

(IV) BUSINESS, CONTRACTS, TRADE, AND TRANSACTIONS.

(V) STATE AND GOVERNMENT.

(VI) INTERNATIONAL RELATIONS, I.E., (I) *DAWAH* AND (II) JIHAD.

Humans by nature are very animalistic and have strong desires. They can figure out ways to fulfill those desires, and when they become angry because of those desires, they tend to retaliate and defend them as well. All these are in their nature and Islam does not seek to subdue or kill that innate nature, but rather it polishes it and civilizes it, and if it gets out of hand than Islam controls it. For this control, Islam gave us the concept of a state as we mentioned before. However, a state, just like an individual, cannot exist in isolation and loneliness; it must maintain relations with other countries, even with those states that are not Islamic.

THE BASIC PRINCIPLES IN THIS REGARD ARE:

(I) THE VERSE OF SURAH MUMTAHINAH:

"Allah does not forbid you of those who did not fight against you on account of Deen and did not drive you out of your homes to do kindness to them and to do justice to them, Verily Allah likes those who do justice. Indeed, He forbids you of those who fought against you on account of Deen, drove you out of your homes and helped to drive you out, to befriend them, and whosoever will befriend them, they are the wrongdoers." - (60:8-9)

These are the principles that no enmity should be done with non-enemies. Rather they should be dealt with kindness and justice, as that will be accessed to convince them to accept Islam. That is the fundamental duty of the *Ummah* of Muhammad, to call towards Islam, but there is no room for friendship with those who have shown their enmity to Muslims because of their *Deen*.

Allah said:

> 1. *"O you who believe! Take not my enemy and your enemies as friends." -(60:1)*

This verse made it clear that the enemy of Allah must be dealt as an enemy of Islam and Muslim so the Muslims may not befriend them.

Allah said:

> 2. *"Let not the believers take the disbelievers as friends [or protectors] besides/against the believers and whosoever will do that has nothing [considerable relation] with Allah except if you protect [yourselves] from them as a protection, and Allah warns you of Himself and to Allah is the final return." - (3:28)*

3. *"O you who believe! Take not* Bitanah *beside you [or against yourselves], as they will not fall short of inflicting insanity in you. They wish to harm you severely. Hatred is already appeased from their mouths and what their breasts [hearts] conceal is much worse." - (3:118)*

"O you who believe! Take not the disbelievers as friends besides (against) the believers." - (4:144)

4. *"O you who believe! Take not the Jews and Christians as friends. They are friends of one another." - (5:51)*

5. *"O you who believe! Take not as friends those who take your Deen as a mockery and fun among those who received the Scripture before you." - (5:57)*

In verse number 2 and 3 the statement "beside or against you" means that any friendship with them, which goes against Islam and Muslims, is prohibited. In verse number 5 it mentions those who take your *Deen* as fun and a mockery. So, you may not befriend them because *Deen* is a very sensitive issue, and if someone will laugh at it, it harms your sentiments and feelings, and a reaction is expected. The reaction towards you friend will be harsher than against one who is not your friend, so it is best not to befriend such people to avoid that terrible situation.

Then another verse made it even clearer:

"Verily those who believed and emigrated and strove hard [fought] with their wealth and their lives in the cause of Allah as well as those who gave them asylum and help, they [all] are friends [allies] to one another. Moreover, as to those who believed but did not emigrate [to the Islamic state of Medina] you owe on the

duty of protection to them until they emigrate. However, if they asked your help in Deen *then you owe the duty to help but not against people with whom you have a treaty (bond), and Allah is all-seer of what you do." - (8:72)*

This verse said:

(I) The Muslim must protect and befriend one another, and the Islamic state must protect their citizens (even non-Muslim citizens) by every possible means.

(II) The Islamic state does not owe any duty to those Muslims who live in non-Muslim countries, as they are neither citizens nor subjects of the Islamic state.

(III) Yes, in *Deen* if they seek any help then the Islamic state may help them as the building of a Masjid, religious institution, literature, et cetera. However, if that help is requested for another thing like fighting, then if there is any treaty with that non-Muslim state, the Islamic state may not step into war. However, it may tackle the issue with them directly or through a common forum they have. Direct action is a breach of the treaty and if the issue of those Muslims has nothing to do with *Deen*, directly or indirectly, if they even ask for help, the Islamic state does not owe them any Islamic duty. Humanitarian duty is another matter, however; if their human rights are being violated, this is not directly related to *Deen*.

Then in another verse Allah said:

"*And those who disbelieved, they are the friends [allies] of one another. If you [people] will not do that there will be a [big]* fitnah *[oppression] in the earth and a big* Fasad *[disorder, mischief]." - (8:73)*

The indication "that" is towards the whole concept mentioned in the aforesaid verse as a whole, the way it is mentioned, the relation with a non-Muslim state is allowed, but rather a must, as the whole world is one human community and nowadays that has become a global village, but this relation must be:

(A) ON EQUAL BASIS BECAUSE A STATE IS A STATE WHETHER IT BE BIG OR SMALL, POOR OR WEALTHY, ADVANCED OR BACKWARD.

This is law and a legal concept, as a human being is a human being, whether he is normal or abnormal, tall, or short, black, or white.

(B) THIS RELATION MAY BE BASED ON TRUTHFULNESS AND JUSTICE, AS TRUTH IS A MUST IN ISLAM, AND JUSTICE TO ALL IS REQUIRED AS ALLAH SAID:

(C) *"Then we pray for the curse of Allah upon those who lie." (3:61) Also,*

Allah said:

"Be just that is nearer to piety." (5:8)

(D) THIS RELATION MAY NOT BE AGAINST THE QURAN AND SUNNAH

As Allah said:

"It is not for a believing man or woman when Allah and his Messenger have decreed [or revealed] a matter that they will have any option in their matter and

whoever disobeys Allah and his Messenger, he has indeed strayed in a plain error." - (33:36)

"Say, if your fathers, your sons, your brothers, your spouses, your kindred; the wealth you have earned, the commerce you fear a decline, the houses in which you delight are dearer to you than Allah and his Messenger and then Jihad in the causes of Allah, then wait until Allah brings about his decision." - (9:24)

These eight things are the ultimate priorities for a human being, but Allah and his Messenger and Jihad are prior to all these so that nothing could be given priority against Allah and his Messenger, i.e., his *Deen*.

(E) FULFILLMENT OF PROMISES AND HONORING THE TREATIES.

Allah said:

"O you who believe! Fulfill your obligations." - (5:1)

"And fulfill the covenant. Verily the covenant will be questioned about." - (17:34)

Yes, if there are enough signs that they are going to cheat the covenant then make it clear to them, and if there is sufficient proof that they want to do that, then inform them and give them time that from such and such date that the covenant is gone.

"And if you fear treachery from a people then throw back to them [their covenant] on an equal basis." - (8:58)

"But those of the idolaters with whom you have a treaty and who have not subsequently failed in aught,

nor have supported anyone against you so fulfill their treaty to them to the end of their term." - (9:4)

So, when their treaty of peace with them is binding like this, what about other treaties?

(F) TO LIVE IN PEACE WITH ALL AS LONG AS THEY HAVE NOT SHOWN AGGRESSION, SEDITION, OR CONSPIRACY AND EVEN IF THE WAR WITH THEM STARTED, BUT THEY INCLINED TO A PEACE TREATY, THEN THE MUSLIMS MAY INCLINE TO IT IN THE SAME WAY.

"And if they inclined to peace, then you may incline to that and put your trust in Allah." - (8:61)

There was a treaty between Muawiya and the Romans. However, Muawiya started his march towards Rome when the time of the treaty is over. He was prepared to launch a fight against them; suddenly an old man on a horse came down the road shouting, "Keep the promise and no cheating." The Prophet said, "Whoever has a treaty with a people so he should not untie a knot nor he should tie it until the term is completed, or he may throw it to them, but on equal basis". This message came to Muawiya, so he pulled back from attacking Rome. That old man was Amr Ibn Anbasah (Ahmad, Abu Dawud, Tirmizi).

(VI) Not to break a trust with them. Allah said:

"O you who believe! Betray not Allah and his Messenger nor betray knowingly your [matters you are entrusted to]." - (8:27)

The jurists of Islam have written not just chapters but whole books about this subject, like *As Siyar*. Like Imam Muhammad, the student of Abu Hanifa has written two books on the same subject. One is concise way and the other is detailed. A non-Muslim from Europe, while studying that book, exclaimed, "O my God! This is the work of the junior Muhammad, what about the senior Muhammad?" His inquiries led him to convert to Islam.

REMOVAL OF *KHALIFA*

The rule of a Khalifa can end:

WITH HIS DEATH

there is no term limit for a *Khalifa* in Islam. Yes, if the *Ahlul Halli Wal Aqd* and the *Ahlul Shura* agree upon some rule in this regard to putting a time limit on it then we think Islam has not prohibited that, but it may be done as a constitutional law.

WITH HIS RESIGNATION

as this is not his personal duty, he cannot be forced into it at the very beginning if he does not want to, nor he can be forced to continue if he changes his mind after being appointed. However, there must be someone to become Khalifa in the proper procedure or as a necessity. For the said purpose, the *Ahlul Halli Wal Aqd* may have someone in mind from before that if something happens. Alternatively, the *Wazeerut Tafweed* (if there is any) will be the Khalifa temporarily or permanently. So, there may not be any vacuum or even the Khalifa himself can do this. However, nowadays there are already laws made in every country that such and such person (by rank) will take over as acting Khalifa.

WITH REMOVAL

The Khalifa could be removed because of two things, as Imam Mawardi mentioned

(I) *Fisq*: If he has become a *Fasiq* (not a just person that is required in a *Khalifa*) but *Fisq* of two types;

i. If he starts following his whims and desires and doing unlawful things, then he is not qualified for the post anymore unless he changes himself again in the proper way and becomes just and *Adl* once more. Then, according to some scholars, he can remain as *Khalifa*, while according to other scholars he needs a new *Bai'at* of *Ahlul Halli Wal Aqd*. Moreover, according to Imam Abu Yala, if a *Fasiq* has been selected by *Ahlul Halli Wal Aqd* to the post in the proper way, his rule is lawful (Al Ahkam). This is like what the Hanafis said, that a judge might be just and *Adl*, but if the *Khalifa* or the ruler appointed a *Fasiq* as a judge, then that is also acceptable.

ii. "Bid'at" in belief- if he has a specific belief but has his interpretation in this regard. However, the very belief of his in that issue is similar to the majority of Ahlul Sunnah, and then there are two opinions

a. REMOVAL,

b. NO REMOVAL AND DEPOSITION.

DEFECT IN BODY

This is of three types,

a) Defect in senses, this is also of three kinds: someone,

(I) If he has lost his inner sense and intellect or lost his eyesight (blindness, not mere nearsightedness, or farsightedness). Such a person does not qualify for *Khalafah* and cannot remain as Khalifa.

(II) If someone has lost his sense of smell or taste, this is not a hurdle for Khalafah neither from the very beginning of it nor if it continues.

(III) If he has lost his speech or hearing, for this there are two opinions. The preferred opinion is that he may not be nominated for *Khalafah*, but if he lost it when he was a *Khalifa* then this case of *Khalafah* may be studied thoroughly. Because it will be difficult for him to understand others due to being deaf and it will be difficult for others to understand due to him being mute. Yes, he can use writing to communicate, and things may be given in writing, but if people do not take him seriously, or they are not afraid of him, then he should be removed.

(A) LOSS OF ORGANS

This is of four types:

a. The loss of an organ that is not a hurdle for *Khalafah* neither in nomination nor continuation, for example, if his ear is cut.

b. The loss of an organ that is a hurdle for both nomination and continuation, because he cannot carry on his duties easily, such as if both his hands are amputated.

c. The loss of an organ that is a hurdle for the nomination, but not in continuation, like if one of his hands is cut amputated.

d. The loss which. In this situation there are two points of views as that is not a hurdle to his performance. However, it maybe upsetting in appearance, such as if his nose is cut. Some scholars said he should not be nominated for the post while some others said he could be nominated.

(B) DEFECT IN PERFORMANCE

(I) It means that some of his subordinates have control over him to such an extent that they implement and execute what they want to, but if it is not wrongdoing, violations, or illegal things then this is not a hurdle for him being *Khalifa*.

(II) If the enemy overtook and imprisoned him in such a way that there is no way of release and acquitting him. Then that is the end to his *Khalafah*. If he is not imprisoned, or he can get out very easily, then he may continue as the *Khalifa*, but someone may take care of the state affairs on his behalf. In the last two cases, the first one cannot appoint his successor because he has lost the authority while the second one can do that and remain as the *Khalifa*.

In brief, we can say that to nominate and elect a *Khalifa* is a difficult job. However, to depose and remove him is even more difficult as most of the time it leads to bloodshed, disorder, and anarchy. Peace and order are the first aims of the government, so his deposition and removal will be legal:

i. When he goes against the Quran and Sunnah openly.

ii. When the advantages of his removal are greater than his *Khalafah* or the disadvantages of his *Khalafah* are greater than his removal because Islam originally orders for a certain thing to have advantages greater than disadvantages or at least allow it.

Imam Abu Yala in his book *Al Ahkamus - Sultaniyyah* said that *Fisq* of both types (as we have mentioned) is not a hurdle either to nomination or continuation. Loss of one's mind (insanity), then that is also not a hurdle for both if it is temporary. However, permanent insanity is a sufficient hurdle for both.

Being deaf or mute or being both deaf and mute is a hurdle for the nomination, but not for continuity of *Khalafah*; but to some scholars such disabilities are a hurdle for continuation as well.

Hafiz Ibn Hazm said,

> *If he is doing wrong to his fellow citizens, so he may be advised not to do that, and if he stopped, then he can remain as Khalifa otherwise he must be removed (Al Fasl).*

Imam Shafi said,

> *He may be removed because of Fisq and injustice to the public. (Sharul Aqa'id).*

Imam Baqilani also said

> *That because of suspending the Islamic punishments, Fisq, injustices to people, oppression, destroying people's lives and properties, not praying, and calling towards not praying is sufficient reason for his removal (Al Tamheed).*

Allama Qurtubi in his *Tafseer* said that lack of belief, not praying, and calling to it is enough of a reason for his deposition.

Obadah narrated from the Prophet not to dispute with the Khalifa in the matters (of *Khalafah*) unless you see an open disbelief of him (Bukhari, Muslim).

Also, Imam Muslim narrated from Auf Ibn Malik that the Prophet said, your best Imams are those whom you like, and who like you, you pray for them, and they pray for you; while your worst Imams are those whom you dislike, and they dislike you, you curse them, and they curse you. Auf said "we asked him should we depose them? He said no! As long as he establishes the prayer amongst you."

Allama Aamidi in his book "Abkarul Afkar" said that to appoint a *Khalifa* is the right of the *ummah*. So, to remove him is also their right, but if the struggle for his removal brings something much worse, they know that they should not try to depose him, because whenever there are two evils so one should choose the lesser of them.

So, the Islamic system is a natural order given by the sole creator and Lord of the entire world, who knows the qualities, needs, and shortcomings of his creature in every time. Only this system can bring peace to the world and safeguard the rights of the people.

MAY ALLAH GUIDE THE WHOLE WORLD AND US TO THE RIGHT PATH. AMIN!

BOOKS BY *QAZI FAZL ULLAH*

Qazi Fazl Ullah has written other books. Below is a short list with summaries.

FIQH KEE TAREEKH WA IRTIQA (URDU)

Islam is *Deen* (religion) and is a complete code of life. Its laws are of two types, textual and deduced, but how the text is interpreted and how laws are deduced therefrom is called *"Jurisprudence"* and the laws are called *Fiqh,* and how this *Fiqh* got developed and compiled. This book gives the details about its stages of development.

MOHAMMADUR RASOOLULLAH (URDU)

The biography of the *Prophet Muhammad* was preserved from day one by his blessed companions. Then scholars and historians have written books in this regard in different times, both concise and detailed. This book on the biography of *Prophet Muhammad* is an excellent balance of concise and detailed, as a concise a book sometimes misses things, and people do not have time to read and understand too detailed a book. Another important feature of this book is that almost with every important part of the *Prophet's* biography, the relevant part of the *Holy Quran* has been quoted, which illustrates that the *Prophet's* life was the practical shape of the *Holy Book*.

SARMAYA DARANA NIZAM ISHTIRAKIYAT AUR ISLAM (URDU)

Humans, throughout their history, have thought ahead and planned their economics and economical needs. They created systems for these purposes. The three systems most widely practiced in history are capitalism, communism, and *Islam*. This book is a comparative study of these 3 economical systems and it proves that the *Islamic* system bestowed upon us by the Creator is the best one regarding justice and no room for exploitation.

DAWAT O JIHAD (URDU)

The basic duty of every *Prophet* and his followers was and is to call the people towards *Allah* in a peaceful, attractive, and convincing way, and wherever and whenever they encounter resistance and hindrances in this regard, they must remove these hindrances. At times, this leads to fights, as when the conspiracy is big and the opponents try to take away their fundamental rights, so they have the right to defend it but how, when, and where? In this book, it is mentioned that *Islam* teaches us to convey, convince, and convert, but not to coerce. This book is an answer to anti-*Islamic* propaganda, especially about the concept of *Jihad* in *Islam*.

ISLAM AUR SIYASAT (URDU)

Islam and Politics—as it is known from the title that this book discusses *Islamic* political system, because *Islam* is *Deen*, meaning a complete code of life and not a set of a few rituals. It has its own system for state and government. So, wherever *Muslims* are in power, if they will implement this system, they meet the needs of everyone, regardless of color, caste, or religion. *Islam* covers the details, such as how to elect a government, and how to run the state to provide peace and justice to all.

RIYASATI ISLAMI KA TASWWAR (URDU)

The title means the concept of an *Islamic* state, and *"concept"* means its conduct. In this book, it is mentioned how and why a state and government is needed, and how that state and government may be and should be run. The Creator *Allah* the Almighty knows all our needs, necessities, qualities, and shortcomings, so the system he has given is the only system that can ensure people's security and safety and can provide them peace and justice, making the state a welfare state.

USOOLUT - TAFSEER (ARABIC)

Every branch of science has its own rules, principles, and methodologies, which provide guidelines for explaining it and how to interpret it, so this methodology is a circle or limits one may keep himself confines to, so he will not get lost or go astray.

This book covers the explanation of the *Holy Quran*, the last and final book of *Allah*. The book of *Allah* is the basic source of *Islam* and *Islamic* law, so its explanation requires certain rules to be followed in its explanation, so one may not be unbridled and without restraint, otherwise he will put his faith in danger.

DIRAYATUR RIWAYAH *(ARABIC)*

Hadith (sayings, actions, and sanctions) of *Prophet Muhammad* is the second fundamental source of *Islam* and *Islamic* laws and also it is the interpretation of the *Holy Quran*. The companions of the *Prophet Muhammad* have preserved them in their memories and in their scriptures and the second and third generation took it from them and preserved them as well. Later, when there was a fear of perversion, then these *Ahadith* were compiled officially and later on, the authentic scholars gathered them together in various books. Furthermore, critics compiled a biography of all these narrators and put certain rules about how a *Hadith* could be accepted. This book includes all these details.

HUJJIYATI HADITH *(URDU)*

This book is regarding the authenticity of *Hadith* of the *Prophet*, as there is a baseless propaganda that *Hadith* were not written in the time of the *Prophet*, but later, making them unreliable. This is wrong, as *Sahaba* used to write *Ahadith* and sometimes the *Prophet* himself used to order them to write. But they trusted their memory more than writing. Official compilation took place later, when *Muslim* rulers became aware of the weakness of people's memories and the loss of those individuals writing. This book provides all these details and makes it clear that *Hadith* is *Wahi* (Revelation) and source of *Islamic Shariah* (Law).

FUNDAMENTALISM, SECULARISM AUR ISLAM (URDU)

Propaganda is being spread either because of ignorance or with mala fide intention that *Islam* is fundamentalism.

Fundamentalism was a term used for Christianity when it blocked the ways of scientific research, invention and development, and some people wanted to adopt it as a basic guideline for states and government. So those who were with research and development branded that as fundamentalism. But *Islam* does not stop or block progress and research; rather, it encourages it and even orders scholars to go ahead and do research, as discussed in this book.

AL IJTIHADU WAT TAQLEED (URDU)

Humans are social and intellectual animals. They have all the same needs as animals, but they are distinct from them because of their intellect as they are looking for their ease, to do a little and get a lot. For this purpose, some intellectuals invent things and others follow them. Then as they are bound to obey the *Deen* of *Allah*, there are other intellectuals who deduce laws from its fundamental sources: the *Quran* and the *Sunnah*, and the less intellectuals follow them, as they should. This is the only intellectual and reasonable way. This book explains this issue and its importance.

MUSALMAN AURAT (URDU)

Allah created the world. He created humans and made them men and women. He gave different qualities to both genders for the smooth running of this life to depend upon each other, but as humans they are equal. Some women made history and they did memorable work that many men could not have done. This small book mentions some of the great work of some great women, particularly *Muslim* women, to make it clear that *Islam* deeply respects women and appreciates their contributions to society.

ASMATI RASOOL OR ZAWAJI AAISHA (URDU)

This world is a combination of opposites and some people have been given a great status. The messengers of *Allah* are the chosen and beloved of *Allah*. He made them and built them up for himself and his work. They are the most respected and honored people, and they must be given respect, as any disgrace to them can harm the feelings and sentiments of their followers, which can cause trouble. In this book this issue is discussed, as well as a misconception about the *Prophet's* marriage to *Aaisha*; namely, that she was minor at that time. Academically and research fully, this book corrects this misconception.

AL FARA'ID FIL AQA'ID (ARABIC)

Aqeedah and *Aqa'id* means faith and beliefs, respectively, and they are the base of *Deen*. Certain beliefs are the contents of *Iman*. What is important for a *Muslim* to believe? These are detailed in this concise book. Some *Muslim* sects have misconstrued some of these beliefs, so the book mentions that as well and makes the right faith clear.

QAWA'IDUT - TAJWEED (ARABIC)

One of the basic duties of the *Prophet* was to teach his followers how to recite the holy book properly. His *Sahabah* learnt it from him and then this became a specific science in future generations. They not only taught their students the proper way of recitation, but they also wrote books about it. This science is called *Tajweed*, which literally means to make good, but in this science, it means to recite good. This book prescribes the basic rules for *Tajweed* as proper pronunciation not only makes the words and sounds good but also helps in giving the proper meaning of the word.

AL QAWA'IDUL FIQHIYAH (ARABIC)

Islam is *Deen* and a complete system and code of life. For each aspect of life there are rules and laws in *Islam*. Some of these rules are in text of the *Quran* and the *Sunnah*, while some others are deduced therefrom. For deduction, the authentic jurists have laid down rules of deduction and the qualities required for themselves. Then, after deduction, they have found some commonalities in different laws in different chapters, so they laid down a common rule for that and these rules called *Al Qawa'idul - Fiqhiyah*, or legal maxims, which make the study of *Fiqh* easy and understandable. This book includes some known and famous legal maxims in all four schools of jurisprudence.

AL JIHAD FIL ISLAM (ARABIC)

Jihad is a very important issue in *Islam*; to defend life, property, honor, and faith is not only a well-known right in each and every culture but also a duty in *Islam*, but how and when? This book is written on this subject; and as this issue is quite controversial, this is a reasonable answer to these questions in the light of the *Quran* and *Sunnah*.

MAULANA UBAIDULLAH SINDHI (URDU)

Maulana Ubaidullah Sindhi, originally from a *Sikh* family, accepted *Islam* when he was a teenager. He studied *Deen* in the proper and traditional way, then joined the freedom movement. He went through a lot of difficulties and lived in exile for 24 years. As a revolutionary leader, he is controversial and many people wrote against him as well as for him. This book describes his personality, struggle, and thoughts to know who he was and how he was.

ASMATI RASOOL AND KHATMI NUBUWWAT (URDU)

Asmati Rasool and *Khatmi Nubuwwat* are reasonable and logical. This book consists of two parts. The defense of the *Prophet* and that of him being the last and final *Prophet* of *Allah* is a reasonable and logical thing, as *Allah* sent messengers in different times to different areas and different nations, and when they worked in their respected times in those areas, *Allah* sent the *Prophet Muhammad* to the entire world to combine their work and bring humanity together on the same theme, subject and faith that all those earlier messengers were sent for. This book is a concise, detailed, and logical interpretation of this finality.

SAYYIDAH AAISHA'S AGE AT MARRIAGE (ENGLISH)

Islam is a Natural *Deen* or *Deen* of Nature. This is a balanced *Deen* providing a comprehensive justice system, and the *Holy Prophet* is the perfect role model as a perfect human. His words, actions, and sanctions are the proper interpretation of the *Holy Quran* and the second fundamental source of laws in *Islam*. There is a commonly held belief, especially among critics of *Islam*, that the *Prophet* married *Aaisha* when she was only nine years of age. In this book, all the details about this issue are given that how this word *Tis'aa* (which means nine) happened there and what the real story is to counter the false accounts and correct the record.

JIHAD IN ISLAM : WHY, HOW, AND WHEN? (ENGLISH)

Jihad as a word in *Arabic* means struggle or striving hard, especially for a noble cause, while as a term in *Islam*, it specifically means to fight in the path/cause of *Allah*. But when does this fight happen? When it is inevitable and unavoidable as the very integrity of a state, the lives of its citizens or the very ideology is facing a big danger. But a very baseless smear campaign is going on against *Jihad* and it is branded as a synonym to terrorism, so this book is a must to make the true concept of *Jihad* clear and counter the propaganda.

SHARIA AND POLITICS (ENGLISH)

Islam is *Deen* and *Deen* means a complete system and a perfect code of life as this is given by the very creator of the worlds, who knows all about his creatures, their qualities, and their shortcomings, and can provide a perfect solution to their problems. But unfortunately, some people have been doing wrong in the name of *Khalafat* and presenting their wrong idea as the *Islamic* political system, so there was great need of a book that can present the proper shape of an *Islamic* state and *Islamic* political system given by the Creator; when executed properly, it is a mercy and blessing for the creatures. This book explains this concept clearly.

HAJJ & UMRAH IN ALL FOUR SCHOOLS OF JURISPRUDENCE (ENGLISH)

Hajj (pilgrimage to *Mecca*) is one of the Five Pillars of *Islam* and a very important but a complicated type of *Ibadah* (worship) as *Muslims* from all around the world get together to perform it together. They follow the interpretation of their *Imams* (jurists), sometimes they look at others when they do not perform a specific virtue the way they do, then they think they are doing wrong, which is not so, but all of them are performing correctly according to the interpretation of their *Imams*. This book gives all these details in sequence according to all four *Imams* the *Muslim Ummah* follows.

MOON SIGHTING, SALATUL TARAWEEH AND SALATUL WITR (ENGLISH)

The *Islamic* Calendar is lunar based. It's different *Ibadaat* time is based on moonsighting; the lunar month starts with the new moon. Even though astronomy tells us what day the moon will be born (i.e., new) with perfect accuracy, discerning on which day it will be visible in a specific area is still not accurate. That is why differences in opinion happen all over the world, and should we to go by the calendar or by a sighting?

Also, at *Ramadan*, which is the most important month in *Islam* as a mandatory *Ibadah*, fasting is mandatory as well, but there is an extra, highly recommended *Ibadah*, the *Taraweeh*, but how many *Rakat* should we pray? *Muslims* differ about this. Another important *Ibadah* is *Salat Ul Witr*. We use this prayer all year, but during *Ramadan* this is prayed in *Jama'at* and different *Imams* have different opinions regarding the number of *Rakats* and its procedure. So, this book gives all the details about these three important issues.

SCIENCE OF HADITH (ENGLISH)

Hadith is the second fundamental source of *Islamic* law. They are the words, actions, and sanctions of the *Holy Prophet*. To record all these in memory and writing, to compile it and to record the biography of those narrators who did this great job and this is considered as a miracle of the *Prophet*. But the enemies of *Islam* used to create doubts in this regard. This book is written on this subject, and it is enough an answer to all the objections that people made from different angles.

ABOUT THE AUTHOR

Qazi Fazl Ullah is an American philosopher, linguist, and author. He is *Fazil Wafaqul Madaris* where he studied *Arabic* grammar, *Arabic* literature, *Fiqh*, jurisprudence, logic, philosophy, *Ilmul Kalam, Seerah, Tafseer, Hadith,* and *Islamic* history. He studied at *Peshawar University* and *Islamic University Islamabad* in *Pakistan* and specialized in law, economics, and political science. He has taught all these subjects in *Pakistan* and the United States at different institutions. He was elected as a *National Assembly Parliamentarian* in *Pakistan*. He worked in underserved areas to provide jobs, build infrastructure, schools, museums, public health facilities, and increase communication technologies as the chair of the *Social Action Board*. He has traveled extensively throughout the Middle East, North Africa, Europe, Southeast Asia, North and Central America. He has given seminars in various parts of the world in these subjects. He speaks and has given lectures and seminars in *Urdu, Pashto, Farsi,* English, and *Arabic*. He has published works in *Pashto, Urdu, Arabic,* and English internationally. He has given the complete *Tafsir Ul Quran* in *Pashto* multiple times in *Pakistan*. He has also given *Tafsir Ul Quran* in *Urdu, Pashto,* and English in the United States. It includes *Usul Ul Fiqh, Usul Ul Mirath, Hadith al Qudsi, Hadith an Nabawi* in English on multiple occasions. He considers himself a student to continue acquisitions of knowledge. He is currently leading *Tafsir Ul Quran,*

Usual Al Fiqh, Seerat Un Nabi, Science of Inheritance (*Mirath*) in English and *Al Mukhtar Lil Fatawa, Dirayat Ul Riwaya* in *Arabic* in Los Angeles, California.

www.ingramcontent.com/pod-product-compliance
Lightning Source LLC
Chambersburg PA
CBHW021808220426
43662CB00006B/220